THROUGH THE EYES OF A CHILD TO THE LIFE OF A MAN

OWEN WILLIAMS (ELEMENTOG)

Grosvenor House
Publishing Limited

This book is published by
Grosvenor House Publishing Ltd
Link House
140 The Broadway, Tolworth, Surrey, KT6 7HT.
www.grosvenorhousepublishing.co.uk

A CIP record for this book
is available from the British Library

ISBN 978-1-80381-723-1

I would like to thank from the bottom of my heart those that have supported helped and been there for me and my kids since ..

Charmaine M (Lucks)
Catherine H
Danielle
Carol L
Ian B
Sam J
Tracy W
Jaqueline S
Pikki Head
Gary C
Claire P
Rachel H
Laura H
Alice B
Sue S
Shanty
Wilf
Jad + (Jad's mom)
Jane (old neighbour)
Sandra (old neighbour)
Jade H (old neighbour)

John P
Sue (old neighbour)
Heather
Vanisha P
Sarah R
Kadi
Petra
Luke
Jay
Jack
Patrick C (tricks visuals)
Simon M
Victim support
Homeless shelters
Solicitor who represented me in my case that resulted in my gaining full PR custody
Of my children
Sarah Rose
Manisha

And Most importantly I'd like to thank my mom and dad for making me the person I am ....

Introduction

It is funny because when your born your born with A sense of innocence, your mind is clear your soul is clean in fact most things if not everything is identified through smell, touch, temperature and sound until you are at a stage where you start to understand things and start to understand life through your own perspective...

This is where I started to understand my life!

Chapter 1

Early Adolescent

I was born @11:30 on 29:07:1979 at Marston green hospital in Birmingham I weighed 5.4oz and was born with an extra finger, (sixth finger) it was half the size as my normal fingers but it use to stick out on the end of my little finger on my right hand, I was born 5 minutes before my brother (my twin) he had breached and mom had already dilated so the nurse had difficulties trying to turn him around into the right position so mom had to give birth to my brother feet first which must had been a really painful experience mom said dad was at the hospital but while being sent to the waiting room the nurse forgot to call him in for the births because it all happened so quickly, but dad must have felt a bit upset, if I were him I would of I felt like they robbed my dad out of the opportunity and experience of seeing his twins being born. We lived in a 3-bed detached house in Birmingham mom me my twin my sister and my older brother. My twin and I were not identical in fact we didn't look alike but people would mistake the 2 of us quite a lot when we were seen individually!

Most of the areas we lived was predominantly white but over the years it had gotten a little better as far as mixed culture. I remember my first experience with racism quite early my mom would send us to the shop and as me and my brother sometimes sister would be walking we would encounter kids chasing us on more than one occasion calling us black bastards and nigga and racial slurs, the first couple of times was really shocking we ran in fear and at times would not like to go to the shop on our own as we never told mom what we was experiencing then one day my oldest brother had found out and went and saw the main ring leader and gave him a beating the guy pulled a knife out but my brother still rendered him and from that day he never did anything

1

like that again in fact in some bizarre way we all actually became friends and ended up joining in and playing football together and borrow computer games off each other, My twin and I shared a room I remember we had bunkbeds I loved being on the top bunk because it meant it was less chance of people sitting on my bed and messing up my blankets, I had a thing about my bed looking messy I always felt better if my bed was made properly, and my blankets wasn't creased. Plus being higher up on the top bunk made me feel like I had my own little bit of space whenever I needed to whine down and just chill out, I would be there chilling writing poetry or writing out of a book or writing some lyrics of from a 2pac song I just loved reading and writing that was something I did with passion. Most of the time my bedroom is where my mom would find me, my mom was a beautiful black queen she always tried her best to install stability and routine in to the house me and my brothers and sister had basic chores to do like made our beds cleaning our rooms and making sure we packed away toys and stuff we had out that day, every couple of weeks we would change the bedroom completely around and it would give the bedroom a new look and made me want to be in my room because it felt comfortable, I think my mom was teaching us independency for later life and tried to install in in all of us from young so we understood that in life nothing gets done if you just sit around doing nothing so I think having so kind of responsibility was more of a positive for me even though at the time chores seemed like punishment at times all the cleaning and lifting and moving stuff but after a while it became the norm. My older brother was cool he didn't really chill with us that much to be honest he was always with his friends.

My twin and I would often play his Atari, and Sega mega drive the Sega mega drive was awesome 2 player games like Donkey Kong double dragon, golden axe, we loved these games as a kid it was something I spent a lot of time on was playing video games with my brothers for hours. Its special having an older brother he kind of did his own thing at home and had his own friends so he didn't really do much as a brother with me unless we were being competitive on a computer game, having an older brother did make me feel secure though as everyone in the area knew him respectively so had respect for me as his younger brother so no one really tried to mess with us either as he had a reputation that didn't need to be explained and being a younger brother I had him on a pedestal like a hero. He had an exceptional natural skill with a pencil my brother could do it all, draw sketch, shade, some of the things I witnessed him sketch were truly amazing. My little sister was a typical little sister she wouldn't allow anyone to go into her bedroom unless she said so and if she found you in her room its was literally the 3rd degree or a complete pat down like I was under arrest but she could enter our room whenever she felt like it, my little sister always got her own way she loved to borrow my 2pac albums and whenever I would try to get them back she would claim that they were hers and she brought them herself I would reply with "how did you buy them" considering you are under the parental guidance" and she would reply sarcastically with "it's mine get out of my room" I would just laugh to myself and get them out of her room when she wasn't there or when she was sleeping, but this would often be a regular back and forth because since she heard me playing 2pac music in my room she became a fan and then claimed that she was his biggest fan but I would not have that and would always tell her that I was but that was just my little sister for you spoilt but loving and caring she would always be in our room when she was bored she would play with her dolls in our room or just do some drawing or playing some game and getting me and my twin involved. My twin some would say was the most mischievous out the 2 of us. My twin and I spent all our time together I mean literally if you saw one you saw the other we were like 2 peas in a pod, we wore the same clothes right down to our vest and socks because dad had a thing about us dressing completely the same from head to toe he would often let us go and get changed if he popped home and we were wearing didn't tops on, we had so much clothes my twin and I had to use the boiler room as our wardrobe where all our clothes were folded on top of each other in two's so it was a case of which ever one of us got dressed first the other would have no choice but to wear the same.

My twin and I were very competitive from press ups to sit ups to computer games to having racing sprints outside, we would often wrestle and had play fights until one of us took the play fighting a little too serious which would lead to mom shouting "stop the bloody fighting up there" it's nice to have the competitiveness of a twin brother because I believe it helps build you up for later life we did so many things together even when the play fights and the squabbling got a little pout of hand it was all in the name of love It was just our way of bonding, being a twin often made me feel like I had more of a responsibility out of the both of us at times as I felt a lot of weight was on my shoulders being 10 minutes older and at times I didn't feel like I had my own identity most times felt like the older brother looking out for the younger brother and it was my job to make sure that he didn't get in to trouble because if he got into trouble then I would it was just so stressful for me at times because I would literally get beaten by my dad if my brother had got into trouble at school then my dad would beat us both even though I was in top sets at school and I was barely never in trouble at school I would still get beaten, I could never understand the logic behind it and all it did start a sense of resentment in me and built up sadness and anger inside at the same time. From my early adolescent I remember both happy and sad times at home. I often heard Mom and Dad arguing and having fallouts mainly over Dad's over friendly relationships with other women. In the line of work Dad did he had many occupations. Honestly, not quite sure what Dad did but, I just know it required being smart, tough and intelligent. It wasn't your typical 9-5 job I'll tell you that Dad kept all of he's personal work away from the family home. Even though we were kids we were not stupid as we got older, I had an idea of the line of work he was in but whatever it was he always provided money for Mom when it came to Birthday's and Christmas he was just never there, I remember mom saving up 50 pence pieces because at the time I remember that was how we had electricity and every couple of months a meter man would come around and empty the meter and mom would get back anything that had been left over after the bill was paid, all I know is that whenever the meter man would leave the table was always full of 50 pence pieces it look like loads of money I remember seeing it at times and thought "wow mom's rich" but to be honest it was probably only £100 lol.

Birthdays were fun! Sharing it with my twin it just made it extra special. Apart from the presents and the fun and suspense of what's behind the wrapping paper, blowing out the candles with everyone you loved singing happy birthday was the best part. I remember wanting a scale electric car racetrack. I remember seeing it on the TV adverts all the time it just looked so cool 2 people can play racing cars round the track together and complete the for the bragging rights. At this age nothing seemed better! My brother and I loved cars! I never quite got the scale electric version it was always sold out by the time Mom went to purchase it, but we got a similar version just a different brand from the town market. (Latiffs) We had fun with it anyway. What I always wanted was a bike but I it was never something that my parents managed to obtain but we got the nearest thing which was a skateboard which I ended up crashing into my brother with and he hit the floor head first and had to have a cap on his tooth I was really upset and my mom and my brother was too I felt really bad because it was my fault that he would have to have a permanent cap on the front of his tooth because of me! I don't remember opening presents with Dad on my Birthday Mom would say he was away on business, or maybe that was just an excuse? But to hear him sing Happy Birthday would have made my Birthday perfect. Those were the things that seem matter more to me at the time, and the love so it would always be a memory, but it was a regular occurrence so over the years we just got used it. Bedtime was the time it would affect me the most where I would lie there on my top bunk and just sit and think about why dad wasn't ever here every day or why he was never here to watch me open birthday or Christmas presents along with other things like walk me to school or come and watch me play in the school football team or just being here so I could tell him how well I was doing at maths because in school I was pretty good at maths, some nights I would wet the bed with all this thinking and stuff that I use to bottle up inside I remember wetting the bed on a few occasion which wasn't a good thing as I would have to strip all the bed and have to have a full bed change which did lead to a telling off from mom more out of frustration I was only a small child at birth being only just over 5 pounds but I was a good sleeper mom said I was never any trouble once I had the breast milk I slept well. many times, I heard mom crying in the other room after shouting and swearing in the house it used to frighten me, I couldn't wait sometimes for it all to just stop and then finally when it did the atmosphere in the house was just different. I remember my dad would make me and my twin jog on the spot for about an hour and do press ups and sit ups In between continuously even if he wasn't there, he would have our sister watch us to make sure that we were carrying out the routine he had set. I guess this was just my dad's way of building us up into strong young men. We didn't really go to friends' houses unless it was our friends carl and Paul who lived a couple of doors down they had an older brother called mark but being much older he didn't hand with us carl and Paul use to always be at our house playing computer we us to have streetfighter competitions and it was some of the best times of fun I had because again we were all competitive but I would say I was one of the best at streetfighter we had some real all night battles on that game Paul would usually be with my older brother along with his others friends at the time that were Danny, shandy, Julian and edamame they were like the click suit gang because at the time the fashion was click suits and all my friends had them they really set a trend as far as fashion, they use to play basketball and they were really good at it but I would say Paul and my older brother were the best out the bunch me and my twin use to sometimes sit and watch them play, I wasn't that good at basketball but I would give it a go sometimes but I was more a football fanatic whenever we weren't playing computer and stuff we would have pillow fights I mean literally turn the lights out in the bedroom and everyone would be swinging and times there were some serious bumps and bruises if one of us ended up crying we would be praying to god that mom didn't hear us or we would have been in serious trouble but we were boys being boys.

This is my mom as a 10 yrs old ... she is so beautiful I feel that I lost out on so much about myself after mom left that I forgot who I actually came from but this is my mom, she went through so much as a young women raising 4 kids practically on her own for whatever reasons my mom left and didn't return but respectfully only my mom knows .. but as for me as a child that witnessed the abuse what my mom suffered I can only hail my mom as a complete hero and an inspiration I remember coming home seeing mom in bed with tablets everywhere thinking mom had took an overdose I panicked and we called her friend at the time Irene and she came and some how managed to wake my mom up I was frightened that day I really thought mom had decided that she had had enough of the mental n physical abuse .. my mom was held down and had all her hair shaven off while under the threat of being executed in front of ppl that should of saved her but they were too scared I would never have let that happen to her no matter how big or small I was .. that is something I could never forgive or forget especially when years later you hear the person glorifying and constantly talking down about it like my mom is worthless and for me it was disrespectful and that's when I realise a line has to be drawn it's not that I'm picking sides between my mom and dad but mom should never have had to experience this life and I wanted her to know that now I'm older I don't blame you I understand .. I know one thing is that I know my mom loved me she just wasn't around to tell me that enough .... but she is a survivor.

I have since found my mom after 30 years and we have reunited I can't tell you how it feels it's just emotions after emotions but I wanted my mom to be seen in the light she should be and not someone who just walked out on her kids for a easy life my mom is hard working she has complete many courses at university and is in charge of a whole floor at a dementia home clinic she's really caring and takes pride in her job and loves to help others and I'm proud of her .. I love you mom x.

CHAPTER 2

SCHOOL YEARS

At 14 I was into football I used to support Leeds UTD. I remember the year we won the Championship, back then it was the equivalent to what now is the premier league. My favourite Leeds players were Eric Cantona, Lee Chapman and Gordan Strachan. My Mom used to buy me the match book every Tuesday from the local shop she used to work in. and get posters, stickers and general information on football. It seemed the best thing ever at the time I looked forwards to Tuesday's as I used to take my football cards to school and swap cards with friends, we were all football mad! In class was the same even though I was in top sets most of the time. History just seemed boring. As soon as the teacher finished explaining the work my friends and I would be talking and doing our work at the same time, which usually got us all separated in the classroom on many occasions if was even worse if it was a double lesson the lesson just seemed to drag more but one thing it did do was it made you actually take note of the work that was in front of you more, we always attended school with blazers on I think we were the only ones that did I think you could say that we were trend setters because most teachers would always say that we were smartly dressed they would often comment on how smartly dressed I was every teacher had different methods of punishment some teachers would send you to the unit where you would have to sit in an isolated room and made to write out lines of the same word "I will not" and whatever it was that you were sent to the unit for, my mom would tell me stories about when she was at the same school and how their methods of punishment was different I mean my mom once told me that they would literally get the Kane I mean literally the teacher would Kane their hand I really couldn't see how that would of went down in my generation at school that would of probably caused a riot or a complete shutdown.

Other methods if certain teachers felt necessary, they would call home and ask for parents to come to the school to discuss your behaviour, but I think that happened to me once, but I told my teacher that my mom's phone was broke which then led to a letter home which in soe ways was even worse. I loved being at school it was where I felt like I could be myself find out who I am the things I love doing the things I was good at the things I didn't like and interaction and making friendships and relationships with others. I loved writing, it doesn't matter what it was I would just love writing, my own stuff or writing long paragraphs. School was the place for me but it wasn't good when 2 of your best friends was off sick, the day just seemed to be less interesting the classroom wasn't the same but it made me concentrate more in certain classes where I would be easily distracted or distracting others, I couldn't get to grips with my history lesson even though my teacher was a good teacher it doesn't matter how she explained the work it just seemed like a headache, the only good thing about it was that if she asked if anyone would want to read a chapter on world war 2 I would be the first to raise my hand because reading was something I was passionate about. it didn't matter how many people I had to stand in front of and read I just felt like I was in my element it didn't seem to faze me which is why I loved English because I was always able to read out aloud in class, in almost every lesson plus I found that I understood and took things in more when I read, my English teacher would always encourage me to read she helped uplift and build my confidence as far as reading, with her praise and encouragement she made me feel good about the work I did in class, I remember having a poem I wrote put on the wall in the classroom for everyone to see which was a big confidence booster for me I felt special and had a feeling of acceptance like I belonged here and my work was appreciated.

Dinner times in school was fun we would have to form a line with dinner tickets which at times was complete chaos pushing shoving and just total havoc until the dinner halls doors were closed and everyone was told that if there wasn't a straight line then no one was going in for dinner that usually did the trick because after being stuck in a classroom for 3 hours all everyone wanted at 12:30 was food and drink, my brother sister and I used to be on special dinners in school which meant anytime there was pork on the school menu we would have pizza and chips or burger and chips because my parents had notified the school to tell them that we were allergic to pork but in all honesty they were just against us eating it because my dad was a Rastafarian and respectfully that was our parents culture and its followed me ever since my sister had an egg allergy so she also had other reasons for special dinners, other kids at school got to leave the school premises and go and hang at the local chip shop which was 200 yard from the school but we were never allowed to leave the school premises under no circumstances and it was where most of the fights happened and mischief but to be honest I loved playing football too much and besides sneakily hiding behind the back of the sheds to share a quick cheeky two's on a menthol cigarette with a few mates, my whole lunchtime was spent picking teams and playing football against different form classes in the school tennis courts with my cousin glia Marcus my twin abba Dakin Haines Phillip Daniels Scott martin carl Neville steven Stewart lee Colvin Aaron shaw Vernon Thornton Christian Griffiths Hayley Goodchild craig Hessian Andrew mason Andrew travis Mathew beard gamesy Wayne Golding, Cosgrove they were the best games ever there just wasn't enough time in the lunchtime always guarantee that someone would rip or tear their trousers. School was one big experience you see so much, hear so much and learn so much about yourself. I had 2 crushes in school, "lucy D" and "Amanda H" but the funny thing is my first girlfriend in school was Sally C after saying no a few times, I finally gave in with peer pressure from her friends and mine I remember kissing for the first time in school at the side of C block next to the cdt classroom both standing there getting off with each other, friends whistling while we are caught in the moment hearts raising like we both just got caught committing a crime but that became the ice breaker. I was in 2 of sally c classes which was funny because I remember us sitting next to each other holding hands under the table whilst we were doing work and discreetly kissing every time the teacher turned to write the topic in question on the board, having a girlfriend in school was the only time I really got to see each other as my parents were strict.

I wasn't always aloud out after school I was always in the house with my brother looking after our sister when mom went to work mom would always ask me while she was at work if could make an apple crumble because that was something that she liked and I could make it prefect, in the mornings for school mom would take my sister and me and my brothers would walk to school together - I remember we use to rob steal from the local newsagent shop every other day we would take it in turns to distract the cashier and whoever wasn't would be filling up our bags with sweets chocolates pop and chewing gum we got away with it for a while and we were cool bringing in loads of goodies for everyone to share at school but eventually in the end the inevitable happened and one day we were caught red handed, the shop manager had been watching us all along on camera and was waiting for the right moment to apprehend us as we were only young and plus the manager knew my parents so he let us off with a warning and didn't phone the police but I remember him banning us from entering his shop on our own he was happy for us to attend the shop as long as we were accompanied by an adult. My mom was so upset when she arrived at the shop, she was so embarrassed and ashamed she said "what have you done" I just looked at her with a sad face of guilt, "has a cat got your tongue" she said in a disappointed voice "I can't believe you are stealing wait until you get home" we were made to apologise to the shop manager and walked home with a lot of verbal abuse on the whole journey home, but I think it was justified as it didn't look good and we did embarrass my mom but most of all ourselves, we begged mom not to tell dad and she never as we would have got more than a verbal telling off. after school my brother sister and I would wait in reception until we all arrived and then we would walk home together it was a long walk at times but it didn't seem so long as we spent it talking about the days latest gossip and events that occurred that day at school or we would play spot the bumper car which was a game we would often play where the first person to spot a bumper beetle car would friendly punch the closet person in the arm it was fun it passed the time if we never did that we would often collect fallen conkers from a field we would have to cut through on our journey home, but by the time I got home there were times where I would have a dead arm from all the punches in my arm. once home it was the usual routine say hello to mom and tell her about my day dad was never really their after school either we just presumed he was doing business or something then it was straight upstairs fold trousers over balcony throw dirty shirts n vest socks and boxers in the wash basket while we could smell the foods aroma just drifting around the house, dinner time was nice but also different and strange depending on what you were use to I always use to see families on tv programs happily passing cutlery and plates and helping each other set the dinner table but in our home it was the very opposite, we had tables and chairs they were really classy but we just never sat in them, for dinner don't ask me why we just never did my brother and I would eat our dinner in our rooms on our floor watching tv or playing computer games while we eat but never did we sit at the table like a family after dinner I would be responsible for mainly washing up I was supposed to share days with my older brother but he always managed to swindle out of it as he was out with friends, being the oldest so mom would tell me to do them without moaning which I did, you could say that I did the majority of the washing up in the house, when I wasn't doing chores I was always out shopping with my mom I would be the one that always went shopping and carried moms bags everywhere, if I wasn't doing that then I was playing computer or drawing writing or occasionally playing football outside in front of the house, if I wasn't in the view of eye sight whenever mom would come outside then I would be inside and was in for the rest of the week which would seem like a year sometimes but most of the times I would be out the front playing football with other friends from the estate we lived on so mom never had to send out the search party, if I wanted to go the park I could only go if my neighbours daughter who was a couple of years older was taking us or I wasn't allowed never and mom or dad never took me and my brothers n sister to the park so it was nice to go when we was allowed even thought it was only for 2 hours and when we got near the house we would be met by mom standing at the door as if she had been worried looking out for us like oh there you are.

I really loved my mom she was everything, if I was hurt, I could go to my mom if I needed a hug reassurance or just anything it was my mom that would always feel that I could go to. I remember walking home from my nans one day with my mom and my brothers and sister we had just left my nans house and we were all walking home we didn't live far it was like a nice 20 min walk but it didn't seem that long once we were walking and talking and cut through a few shortcuts. one day on the way home I was hit by a car and never even realised until I tried to take a few more steps and realised that I was walking on adrenaline, I then remember falling to my feet and not being able to actually move another muscle I was still conscious I think I was in complete shock I collapsed which caused a bit of chaos as I was outside a load of local shops so a crowd quickly started gathering. everyone had come out the shops to see what the commotion was, "my leg me leg" mom my leg" I shouted my mom was trying to calm me down and reassure me that the ambulance was on the way and was going to take care of me and that I'm going to be alright, someone who had saw what had happened managed to stop the car from driving off and my uncle who happened to be in the area at the time ended up punching the guy and that caused him to run off in fright there was so much going on in such a short space of time everything just seemed to happen so quickly, it wasn't long before the ambulance arrived and flashing lights and crowds gathering out of nowhere with the most amount of attention I was getting, my mom kept saying you're going to be alright son you're going to be alright, when I finally got to the hospital and was finally seen by the nurse and doctor and after a scan and an x-ray I was told that my right leg had been broken it was the first time that I had broken any bones at all so it was really awkward and painful I had to bear the pain for a while as the tablets I was on wasn't that affective at first and took a while before they actually kicked in it would be hours sometimes so I would spend most of my time in bed writing and resting or watching football my mom was always at my side if I needed anything I saw all the effort my mom made the sweat blood and tears she put in to try to run a stable loving balanced home but I also saw the strain and pain and stress and the pressures of life in her eyes. Whatever I never received in gifts my mom always made up for it in a form of love in fact when I close my eyes and reminisce, not to disrespect my parents because I love them but I don't recall ever a day where we went out as a family or even remember opening Christmas with us all or being festive because dad was always away or too busy doing something it seemed so it was just mom and I and my brothers and sister we would watch cartoons whilst mom would be doing the Christmas dinner trimmings and everything then mom would get all the Christmas decorations out the loft and we would help put them up and around the house while mom was running back and forth around the house trying to make sure that everything was perfect for us when Christmas dinner was ready I remember it being one of the only times we would sit at the dinner table as a family pulling Christmas crackers and putting on Christmas hats and trying to be festive, mom would allow my brothers and I to have a sneaky baby sham which was like a alco pop which made me feel really grown up for the moment, I also learnt what the wishbone was when the turkey was cooked we would making a wish after pulling and breaking the biggest piece of the wishbone at the dinner table. I remember making a wish and wondering how come it hadn't come true when I woke up, I realised how wishing was just a myth and if there was anything learnt was that wishes was only granted in fairy tales. after we would all finish dinner playing with toys and watched cartoons with a full belly we would get washed and dressed and carry on the festive spirit at my nans house so we could see the rest of my family at Christmas plus it was one of the only times we got to see all our cousins together which was always nice. we would have all kinds of fun playing pass the parcel to dance offs laughing and eating food and deserts and just having a good time.

I enjoyed Christmas at nans it was one of the only times when mom seemed really relaxed and in her element throughout the Christmas season, it seemed to go so quickly before I knew it I was back in school in a double history lesson getting told off for talking about what I had for Christmas, football or some new lyrics that I had just finished writing and wanted to know what my friends thought of them. About 6 months after my leg had healed I was able to go back to school and was fit enough to get back to playing football, So it was only inevitable that I would be in the school football team which was one of the highlights of my school life for me, my pe teachers Mr Gordon and Mr price were my coaches and they help build my confidence and encouraged me enough for me to believe in my own ability and started to take football seriously but everything was about my behaviour in school, like if I was going to represent the school then it came with a level of responsibility in school my lessons I was in would have to keep my pe teachers up to date with my attitude in school lessons and how I conducted myself as a role model to some of the younger years. my pe teachers help mould me into the centre forward because of my pace and being one of the fastest in my year at times it was only right that I was used to my full potential sometimes I would be used on the wing also as being left footed after my accident I wasn't really able to use my right leg with the confidence I had before it was broken from the hit and run that's something I kept to myself as I didn't want my opposition to feel like they had an advantage over me on the pitch or in life itself, over time I just learnt to cope with it and put it to the back of my head but it use to really bother me at certain times, I remember scoring goals against most school teams but my favourite was against park hall and Grimshaw because I knew other players from these school so it was like a bit more of a personal competition and made you up your game and there was also a bit of school rivalry then so losing to either of these school teams was a no. I remember a player called big Erol for Grimshaw who was a very good player and before the game I remember our defenders saying we need to watch him as he was their top player he scored that day and it looked as if we were going to lose but I scored the equaliser before the first half and then I managed to get the winner in the second half I felt like a hero it was almost like a cup final I would look over to the side lines and see my mom cheering "woo well done son" with some of the other parents that managed to come to the game, the next day int the school assembly the headmaster would read out the school football and netball results from the evening before and made it his duty to especially call me out to the front to receive a standing ovation from the school because of my winning goals against Grimshaw school, it really grew my confidence but at the moment I was really embarrassed but all my friends were calling my name and saying well done well done which made everyone else join in cheering whistling and clapping until the headmaster would tell everyone "ok everyone now calm down please" it also made me very popular in the school amongst everyone especially with the girls it also made forming friendships and relationships easier because everyone would want to hang out with the team as it was cool I started focusing more in my school classes also not being distracted as much not distracting others and not answering back the teachers but it wasn't something that I found that easy to do but I got much better because as a teenager I had a bit of a chip on my shoulder especially if I was ever challenged or told off I would feel really anxious but I learnt to respect the school rules and policy and managed to adapt and focus to better myself and to stay in the football team because I realised that I had what it took and my pe teachers had put a lot of faith in me and I didn't want to just let myself and them down.

Anytime it was dinner time and we played football in the tennis courts I would always be a different player as in my favourite football players it was something we would all do as friends whenever playing football, sometimes I was Ian wright pele Romario Beppe signori or Bergkamp Andy Cole shearer I would always try to play like the players that I wanted to be it gave me more motivation, I literally lived and breathed football.my mom was the only one that came to watch me play for the school football team and encouraged me to be a footballer she always brought me football magazines and things associated with football any time saw a bargain in the market, I also loved Tae kwon do I remember mom hearing about a class that had started up in castle vale and so I attended with my brothers It was really something that I enjoyed I started off on white belt had a few seminars and competitions and was doing really well I managed to make it to brown belt and the affordability became a problem as it was costly for mom to keep buying all the equipment and pay to enter competitions or to take the next belt upgrade but I learned so much. I remember we had a ceremony for those that had achieved belts or new gradings, so certificates and awards were being given out to acknowledge the accomplishments of those that had impressed. I was called as one of the only people to have correctly answered and understood all the important facts and body parts when using Tae kwon do, I Was so proud of myself and so was my mom I was met with a standing ovation and congratulated by the instructor. "Well done really impressed I'm so proud of you son" said mom then finally all that stopped!

One morning I woke up in the middle of the night it was quite early and I could hear rustling sound like the sound of someone taking out the rubbish bags so I never thought it was nothing because many times I would wake up and hear mom taking out the rubbish ready for the bin men because they came and collected the streets bins at a certain day and time it wasn't until I heard the door slam close and the sound of a car outside my window that I actually decided to take note, as my bedroom window was located at the front of the house if I slept with the window open I could literally hear every car and noise that was outside, I remember peeping through my curtains and seeing my mom getting into a car and someone helping her put some black bags in the boot of a black car, at first I never really expected anything plus I had just woken up and my mind hadn't been in full motion

I stayed at the window looking until the car my mom had just got into had disappeared out of sight and I could no longer see it in my vision it was only until a couple of hours later that I actually realised that mom wasn't coming back to the family home me being so close to my mom made it hard for me to understand, I remember sitting thinking to myself "no mom wouldn't do that she would never leave me she loves me" she must have just gone to nanny's I thought but I was trying to hold on to something in my heart because I didn't want to believe it was true, at night time Is when I would feel the most pain alone on my top bunk crying to myself in agony on my pillow trying hard not to make a sound or make sure no one would hear my sniffles. I never wanted to believe that she was just gone and not coming back at times I don't even know what I felt I just know that the feeling wasn't nice inside there were times were I was so worried as I had not heard off mom in weeks and remember thinking what if something had happened to her I just didn't like how I was feeling inside about the whole situation I was too young to grasp everything at the time but I understood some situations too, I always thought anytime I heard a car pull up or the door knock I would think it was mom returning but it never was most of the time it was either the post man or my mates or some sales man at the door trying to get us to sign up or register for something but most the time we didn't entertain things like that, eventually days went by weeks went by and then months then years until somehow I managed to find the strength to adapt to life without a mom I never realised at the time but I developed abandonment issues but at my age I was looked at as the sensitive kid whenever I would hear a knock on the door I would always think the worse that someone was going to give us some bad news concerning mom but it never was this is just how my mental state was at 14 I was very sensitive with my heart I stopped caring about my future and life I just couldn't get to grips and focus if anyone even mentioned anything about my mom I would feel a sense of anxiety over take me, I wasn't sure what hurt the most mom leaving without actually taking me or mom leaving without actually letting me know. throughout my childhood I would develop a problem within myself not being able to separate the 2 and that would cause me to feel unloved, lost, confused and isolated at times I started suffering from insomnia like I wasn't doing a full night's sleep, negative nightmares that really had me waking up in fear. I was always sad inside but at the age I was no one never understood at the time that I was a kid who was depressed anxious hurt and broken from within hearted. While attending school I tried to hold everything inside, I started smoking the odd cigarette I don't even know what it was because the first time I tried one I thought I was going to die take a drag and a pass my friends said" after a few pulls I coughed up phlegm and my head started spinning" my friends were laughing "ha ha you got head rush its ok you just got head rush" I had to sit down and get some water to get myself together before lunch was over me and a few friends would chip in 50p each and buy a packet of Benson and hedges or sovereign that were £2.20 for 10 but after a while my throat started feeling really harsh so I started smoking menthol cigarettes which were better whenever I took a pull on them they were less harsh and had a mint taste that had me addicted for a few months but in some way it just felt cool to do plus some of my friends did it too so I guess at the time it felt ok.

Most of my friends at school never lived with both parents so it was quite natural in the aspects of who's eyes your looking at it through but the majority either had both parents at home or just lived with their mothers I was actually now in none of the above, my final years in school was year 10, I didn't actually make it to year 11 as my dad thought it was better to take me out of school in my final year because my twin brother had been permanently excluded and the school had said that they were not willing to take him back in after a violent altercation that had occurred on the school premises which had left another pupil inured, my dad affected me when he did this by somehow thinking that taking me out of school permanently was a bright idea. I was projected to finish with good grades as I was in top sets set 1 In fact, but it's the ifs buts and maybes that I was left with, felt at times that I was being robbed of the opportunity and all the hard work that I put in felt like it was all for nothing all the friendships I built the football team and the whole experience. Just felt like everything I done was for nothing. after applying for every school in the borough and not being excepted I finally signed up for a yts (youth training scheme) where I would go college 4 days out of 5 and on the 5th day I would actually work at the placement because I studied business studies business admin finance my placement was to work as an office junior where I would do database and spreadsheets filing and other general office duties which also required making cups of tea and coffee I really enjoyed myself was overwhelming at times but I met so much people and it helped build my character. I learnt so much. About responsibility and being reliable which was some of the main qualities that was required as far as work and representing the company I was told I always had to be aware of my professionalism. I use to get paid £45:50 every week and I saved that for 3 years only being allowed to take money out for travel expenses as my dad wanted us to save my money, but a couple of years later my dad took me to the bank and withdrew all the savings that I had built up from my yts all them years, I'm not quite sure what he needed it for but I was young and it was my dad asking for it so it was not like I wasn't going to give it to him regardless of what reason it was still my dad so I did what seemed morally right at the time I wasn't sure what he needed the money for and I never asked but all I do know is that my bank balance went from 4 figures to 0 in the space of one transaction I learnt that sometimes in life you just have to accept things for what they are and this was just one of them things that I had to accept, I still was suffering deep inside from mom leaving it was something that I had a problem dealing with from within, one day my uncle p who use to have his giro come to the house was expecting it to arrive one day not knowing that I had obtained it and went and cashed it at the post office don't know what I was thinking I remember back then the giro was like a check that arrived from the government as benefits and you could counter sign it for whoever it was made out to I really regretted it after, it was the one and only time I had ever stolen off a family member and I felt shamed inside I finally owned up to it and my uncle forgave me he was cool like that he use to spend a lot of time with me and my brothers playing computer games having arm wrestles and he always use to train us up with doing press ups and sparring he use to always think he was faster than me but if you ask me I would say he was fast yeah probably a bit faster than me I just never admitted it to him at the time as I would never have heard the; last of it but we were competitive with each other. I respected him a lot for that because he spent his time with me when I needed it most but when my dad found out what I done and I got a complete beat down to the point where I still bare the scar on my left ear to this day but I probably deserved it, I was broken so I ran away for a few months and came back when my uncle s found me and had a chat with me and brought me back home, I just didn't feel right without my mom so many times I would sit in my room thinking to myself "mom mom where are you please mom I need you" but it was as if my cries went unheard, I use to speak a lot to my "auntie S" about everything I was feeling and it helped me to deal with my emotions in fact at the time if I never had her to speak to at the time I would of found it hard to deal with what I was experiencing at the time because she had a way with speaking to me it made me comfortable to open up to her, so I always appreciated that.

Chapter 3

Respect

I started growing up and realised that I wanted to work I just wanted to do something with my spare time that I had, I wanted to put my energy into something because I had a lot of it so one day when I was taking out the bins at my nans my aunties boyfriend who we classed as uncle Roo's had arrived at my nans he just passed by most mornings if he saw my grandads car outside. And always often fixed things that needed fixing in the house he literally could do it all wallpaper plaster flooring fit gas cooker you name it he was the man when it came to things like that, and I respected him for that. One day my grandad had a word with him about how he would feel taking me to work with him to help out the next things I know he asked me if I had got some boots some spare old clothes and a coat and I replied with Yeh sure and that was it that same day I went with him to work, I actually enjoyed the experience, every day without fail before work we would always pull into Greggs and order a pie and a can of orange tango uncle R use to love that its always stuck in my head and he would always talk to me on the journeys about how important it was to have a trade, he would tell me how much studying and how much hard work he did to become a qualified gas engineer fitter. I was so grateful for the experience also and it got me out the house most of the day and I was actually learning something too so I felt like my days were productive, I spent most of the day observing and grabbing the tools out the van and helping screw the bolts off the old fire places and holding and lifting stuff but uncle Roo's would always explain what he was doing or what a certain part was so I could understand. we would have some laughs though it was quite a relaxing and laid back job I felt good when I came back to my nans and my grandad would make me feel like he was proud of me by highlighting that I was working even if it was just a couple of days a week it taught me a lot like time keeping being punctual being professional and conducting myself in the right way like anytime we would step into a customer's house to always use my manners greet them well so the customer would feel at ease. What working with uncle Roo's also did was help prepare me and set me up for when I was going to start a full-time job in the future, and I will always respect him for taking the time out that he did to help try install these attributes in me. At 16 my dad took me and my brothers boxing I remember the first time that I walked into a boxing gym it was in the centre of town in Digbeth by the cauliflower coach station it was run by Robert McCracken it was so noisy there were people working out on the pads, skipping and sparring, I stood there in amazement as I took in the scenery, "are you guys here to train a voice said" yes please my dad introduced us and then left us there and gave us money to make our way home after the session was over, I was really good for my fitness and for my discipline, I really enjoyed it the trainer had a good way of getting the best out of all that attended and he really put me through some workouts drills and techniques "jab jab cross" "jab jab hook" my trainer said as he held up his pads trying to sharpen my arsenal "that's good that's excellent now throw the uppercut in the combo that's good" you're a natural he said I nodded my head and continued like I never heard what he said and continued to work out, after a couple of weeks we had other boxing gyms come and visit the gym and would spar against guys that were in the process of a fight or had one coming up so one day as I was about to hit the pads my trainer had ask me to throw the gloves on and give a guy that had already had a few fights already a spar to sharpen him up "keep the pressure on him my trainer said" turn your punches keep your guard up" "jab use your jab" my trainer was well impressed with me the fact that I had not fought before and just went straight in and gave a guy with experience more than he could handle, in between my rests I would watch Robert spar as he was getting ready for a fight and it was motivating and inspiring to me, Robert would often speak to us when he was free and give us some good tips and advice on boxing it was good to be around a gym that was so professionally run I continued to use the gym and was getting ready for my first real fight but the travel was too far so it became hard to continue so I ended up giving it up but I learnt so much I learnt to defend myself and that boxing is an art and a battle of will, I really wanted to carry on but commitments were taking over and sadly I left the gym. But Robert signed a pair of boxing gloves he had given my twin before we left that we used to use one glove each at home to spar in our back garden and he wished us well with our futures. I reckon had it not been for the commitments and stuff and not really having the support I could have been a good boxer it's something that will always stay with me.

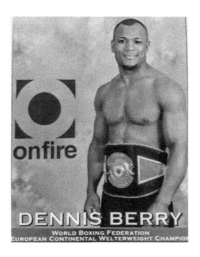

I guess I already had it in my genes as my uncle which is my moms brother was a former World Boxing Federation European Continental Welterweight Champion I never got to watch any of his fights live but I wish I did.

He was very instrumental and inspiring to me in many ways than one ... he understood me differently and gave me his time it don't matter whenever I would call him his always makes time for me whether it was to talk or just to listen and advice me best way he seemed possible I will appreciate that and I respect and love him for that always.

Chapter 4

My First Job

My first job was working at McDonalds I remember I worked on nuggets it was really easy all I had to do was put nuggets in fryer set the timer and when they were done put them into a fresh tray ready to be presented in boxes for order, all I would hear most of the day was "Owen 9 nuggets 6 nuggets 20 nuggets" it was quite fast flowing so once the orders came flooding in I was practically boxing up different portions of nuggets all; day depending on the customers' orders I was so excited when it was my break because I was told that I could literally have what I liked as long as I recorded it in the book the was designed for colleagues so that they could keep a note of the food stock I came into the staff room with 3 burgers 20 nuggets fries milkshake and for the first couple of weeks it was brilliant but then the narrative wore off and I started to get a bit sick of the smell of the food especially McDonald's and there's only so much you can eat in half hour break I would have my family like brothers and sisters putting in orders when I was at work to bring home food and deserts. on a couple of occasions I did when I could but not all the time as I did not want to risk losing my job, I remember I use to be so nervous whenever I was asked to serve on the till and I would see a friend or a family member in the cue and they would automatically give me that look like "oh Owen is on the till so he should be able to sort me some free food" but it didn't always work like that In fact the only time I gave extra food in the bag was when the manager wasn't on the front observing all the orders it was a little bit more easier to get away with it, after about a year I would finally have enough of working in such an environment I was also going to college but also using college of a way of hanging out with my mates because I was never aloud out after school like some of my friends so I would sometimes use my college days to walk around shopping centres getting up to know good with my twin or hanging out in friends' houses if their parents were at work and had a free yard we would play computer smoke weed and raid the cupboards for munchies one day we went to my friend's house who had a free yard I remember use all arriving me my twin and my friend of all of ours we played video games and recall my friend saying he needed the toilet and then then about sometime later my brother did the same I was too busy whooping everybody on the game that I stayed on a winning streak so didn't at any time leave the room at any time for any circumstances ither than when we were all leaving we left in time to line up with the time I would arrive from college so nothing would seem odd when I arrive home to my nan and grandads house everything seemed normal until there was a knock on the door from the police asking for the Williams twins which was my brother and I, I remember many times the police attending our family homes and any time they arrived they would always arrive with about 40 police a lot of commotion and the whole road would be cornered and closed off and you could see the neighbours at their windows peeping though their blinds trying hard not to be seen nosing at the scene which was rather embarrassing I wasn't sure what the police wanted me for I literally thought that the college had called and said that we were missing from class so at first I kind of had the look of guilt on my face when my dad said no not my boys they been to college knowing I hadn't attended. but then I heard the officer say that he was arresting my twin and I for theft and robbery I could not believe what I was hearing I said "robbery what robbery I haven't done no robbery" I remember our dad telling us not to say anything until the solicitor had arrived, and I was put in a van to be taken to the nearest station for questioning when is arrived at the station I was presented with the evidence that was allegedly missing which was £200 which alleged was taken from the parents' bedroom and some sentimental jewellery that I had no idea about knowing I hadn't left the room I was confident enough in myself to know that I couldn't be charged for this also knowing my friends were in the house and they would no doubt be able to vouch for me so I went no comment in my police interview all the way because to me I had nothing to do with whatever they were alleging. After hours in the police station I was released pending further enquiries so I left that day without charge when I returned to the manor word had it that my friends hadn't told the police that I hadn't left the room and that was to the amazement of myself because what that did was allow the police to at least implement that we all had something to do with it when it was nothing of the sort at the time my twin had managed to get himself another charge something completely separate from this alleged incident so with him being on bail my dad thought it was best that I took the charge so that my twin wouldn't be remanded in prison for breaking bail but I explained that I never had nothing to do with it but at the time he wasn't interested he literally told me that I was taking the wrap and that was that. During time, I had to wait for my next court appearance my twin was remanded in custody for bail conditions so on my next court appearance my dad took me to court and told my solicitor that I was taking the wrap for the incident and that I was going to tell the judge today to remand me in custody. I looked at my solicitor and I remember him giving me a look of disbelief that he couldn't believe what he was hearing I had no say in the matter I remember thinking why didn't I just go to college all this because I wagged college, finally I was called up by the judge and through my solicitor he was informed that I was taking full responsibility for the incident.

Chapter 5

Cloth I'm Cut From

The type of family I was from wasn't the average 9-5 workers in fact only my sister and girl cousins and aunties actually worked we were from a street survivor background and that meant we weren't strangers to drama danger and near death experiences our uncle had been shot in the head and managed to survive, also a cousin that had been shot and survived 7 out of 10 brothers had been to prison by 16 I had witnessed family giving family crack and heroine which when I think of it is something I would never do ever, probably the closet I've come to actually being in plain view of almost witnessing a death was a day I would never forget it was a hot day we had a family gathering as we use to do most weekends that involved food and music and good vibes I remember being on the front garden with my brother dad and a few other family members and out of know where a man out of nowhere ran towards the house fired a few shots that were ordered for my brother I remember diving for cover and everyone shouting n screaming my dad I have to say is a soldier just off instinct he went running after the man responsible and drew his weapon and fired but missed it was such a frantic moment. Whatever I say about my dad there's one thing I know and that is that he would throw his life on the line for any of us I witnessed that with my bare eyes on a few occasions to me at the time that was gangster to me. By the time I was 14 police had already knew who I was because of the family cloth that I was cut from so I was already seen as part of a problem because of affiliation, if they just saw us together as a family they immediately suspected we were up to no good, I don't think this helped me as far as being a young kid growing up in an area where you're not given a chance, I was tarnished with the same brush as far as the police were concerned.

Calroy Williams

This is my older brother he showed me how to survive outside, how he moved was important he had a likeable factor to him ppl just seemed to instantly be drawn to him but something I learnt from him was how he was really humble but to look at him you just wouldn't try him on your best day! He had a lot of respect from all over the city because of his realness! I think one of the reasons I was able to maintain in the streets untouched had a lot to do with the street respect my brother had, I mean I could hold my own if it came to it but I feel that having an older brother with the reputation and respect that mine had it helped me to survive in a street full of opportunist! Since my brother came out from doing a long stretch he has since become a Muslim turned his life around and become a Mentor for young ppl, offers 1-1 pt sessions with free consultation and nutritional advice! He also continues to provide for his family and make a positive impact and contributes to charities and society! So for that I will always love and respect my older brother!

CHAPTER 6

FIRST TIME FELON

I was sentenced to 12 months for theft I hadn't took no part in or had no knowledge of, this was the first time I had ever experienced going to prison I didn't know what to expect, I had watched a few prison movies before and saw a few documentaries on jails but I was about to experience it first-hand I had a lot of adrenaline flowing through my body and mind I was quite angry with myself that I was in this situation I eventually made it to glen Parva youth institution prison and was booked in "can u put your clothes in this box and get changed into these "an officer said as he threw me a matching set of grey joggers and a blue t-shirt, "make sure your dressed appropriate he said then he threw me some brown shoes that had no laces in because I came from court in my suit and shoes I never had no footwear that was suitable when I arrived so I had to wear these shoes they were embarrassing, wearing shoes like this is prison just made you look like you were a wuss or you couldn't afford nothing but it was anything but that I finally got on to the wing where I was shown my cell I remember first getting onto the landing and just hearing everyone being loud shouting howling and just all inmates generally being nosey looking waiting to see who was being brought onto the prison wing it was just something that happened in prison it being my first time I didn't really know anyone so when I arrived on to the wing all most of the inmates were concerned about was where I was from and what I was in for I finally was taken to my cell, when I got inside the room I remember thinking is this it is this how smack the room is not only that but I had a cell mate in their also, he stood up when I entered with the officer and introduced himself before the officer left the cell he said "don't kill each other" and walked off with a smug grin on his face with the sound of his keys jangling he then left the room and bolted and locked the door, my cell was about 5ft by 8 ft with one window which was boarded up in like small grids so you couldn't really see out of it but you could open the window as the window had a wire shaped handle that stuck out of the grids that aloud you to open and close it about 3cm just enough for air to be able to get into your room, my cell mate was quite cool he said" is it your first time" I said Yeh" I said "how you know" he said he could tell by the way I had entered the cell that I hadn't been in prison before. he told me he had been in before and told me a few ins and out and what officers to avoid and stuff. But to be honest I just wanted to keep my head down and get my sentence out he way the quickest and easiest way possible. after I put my stuff away and sat on my bed that's when all my emotions came flooding in, I felt like I was crying not only because of where I was but because I had nothing to do with the initial incident but I was the only one being punished for it because all the charges was dropped on everyone else once I was made by my dad to enter a guilty plea after 2 weeks in they brought my twin brother onto the wing and that was good for me he was in prison for a completely different incident and had just been moved onto the same wing as me I asked the S/O if I could be padded up with brother but at first I was told that I would have to fill in an application and would have to wait for an officer to have time to go through it also it depended on my behaviour, having my brother on the wing made me happier and I felt a lot more secure so finally I was padded up with my twin after days of waiting we had joint canteen and was never short of nothing everyone on the wind and landing got to know we were twins and we came quite popular on the wing with the other inmates my twin showed me how to double bubble in prison basically if you gave another inmate a pack a biscuits or Tobacco or anything then you would charge them double back the item it was a way to survive in prison but every now and then you would get that one inmate that didn't want to pay their debt and that would lead to serious consequences where they would be moved off the wing for their safety so you had to be careful because snitching was at an all-time high especially in prison and it wasn't something you wanted to get court up in. I quickly learnt that in prison a situation can go from nothing to something in the flash of a light, compared to the street everything in prison is seen as a violation everyone is sensitive. angry and stressed and being caged up with a bunch of criminals with high testosterone and no release and angry at the system was enough to send some people crazy you literally had to be on you guard at all times, growing from the family I grew from I adapted to life in prison I didn't make it intimidate me I stood strong and gained a nice level of respect I was seen as the reasoning kid cause a few times where my twin had gotten into situations and debates that got silly, inmates would more try reason the problem out with me because my twin was more unpredictable and hot headed, dad had a thing about being each other's shadow he never really saw us as individuals but that's what we were it sometimes made me question being a twin for a moment because I seemed to be punished and mentally stressed from things my twin had done I was also punished for things he did even if I had nothing to do with it and that was affecting the person I was I felt at times like I never had my own life and felt at times like no one understood me, I mean after all its what landed me in prison. at times I was more like the older brother who was here to look after my twin, but in this instance, we were back-to-back all the way all we had in here was each other, the weird thing was no one seemed to look out for me in life I felt like I was responsible for myself and left to find my own way. because I was on remand at the time and awaiting sentencing I would try to get as much character references as I could that would help the judge get a better understanding of me before I would be sentenced. I was finally sentenced to 12 months behind bars. on the day of my sentencing my brother was also up in court for a bail hearing. Because I had already done 6 months on remand, I was released from the court immediately the feeling inside is something I will never forget just the feeling of freedom and relief my brother was denied bail and I was taken back to his cell to get my cuffs off and to say goodbye to him because he was going back to prison, I was just being released. we both hugged and cried our eyes out it's something I will never forget even the officer got emotional, but she gives us the time we needed with each other it was a very emotional encounter I finally let him go and was escorted out the courtroom door to the surprise of some of my family awaiting. "Glad you're out now use your brain and stay out of trouble" that was my auntie that was her way of saying basically get a job and try and do something good with yourself.

Chapter 7

Mental Struggles

I first started having problems mentally around the time of 15 I couldn't control my emotions and many times I sat and thought things through like what the best thing for me was am I even worth being here I wasn't feeling loved, and it seemed whether I did good or not that I would always be punished and most times physical. One day while at home I was questioned by one of my dads girlfriends who was living with us at the time I think it was about 4-5 months after mom had left, she moved in and that's how I met my brother Ls who was 9 at the time but I will explain more about my brother Ls who I love so much later on in the story. Anyway while at home in my room I was asked by her if I knew who this what with that I looked towards her and in her hand was a Picture "here take a look" she said "who is that" I said it's my brother not knowing that she was trying to find out if my dad had another child that she had not known about I answered it's my brother not knowing it was going to lead to a situation that I will never ever be able to get out of my head and my soul! And it started like this!

Later that day an argument between my dad and his girlfriend had started we were all scared not knowing what was going on, we were called down the stairs me my twin my older brother my little sister who was 9 and my brother Ls also when I got down the stairs from this point onwards I will only respectfully describe my ordeal!

I was grabbed by my dad and forced to strip completely naked in front of his girlfriend and those who I mentioned earlier and was beaten with metal bars and sticks until the broke in half

I had urinated and pooed everywhere while screaming in pain shock and agony "dad please" but it continued I felt violated ashamed and embarrassed and completely broken inside and out and numb even as I write this I cry as I relive the ordeal which was not easy to even try and forget that's why I wrote this book it's my way of dealing with the trauma inside even now just thinking about it makes my stomach move in a way that I couldn't describe! at this time in my life the only person that knew I had experienced this was my aunty S without her at this time I would of contemplated suicide but I was just done how fortunate to have her reassure me that I was doing the right thing by telling her and getting it all off my chest so I will always love my aunty S for being their at that stage of my life and I just want to say thank you from my heart if I never got the chance to say it before. I contemplated suicide I contemplated running away I contemplated a lot of things that would just stop me from being hurt and feeling the way I did. I remember on one occasion I stood on the edge of a road and waited and waited for cars to go by in my mind I thought if I just walk out in front of a bus it will all be over all this pain would just go away and I would no longer have to live this way. Eventually I stood in front of a bus and it stopped in front of me and shouted at me "what the hell are you doing get out the road" I stood there and just broke down! the bus had a few people on and at the time I was near a bus stop and 2 ladies had gotten off the bus, one just looked at me like I was out my mind as she crossed over the road to do everything to avoid even trying to encounter with me, the other lady was walking towards me and approached me and said "please may I talk to you with you" whatever is going on In your life is not worth dealing with it this way" she asked if I had parents and to think of the impact that it would have on them she asked me if I had anywhere to go and I just broke down crying she told me to come and have a cup of tea at her home which wasn't far so I eventually found it in me to trust this lady and I agreed to going to her home we spoke for hours I just felt like someone had took time to listen to me and take time to see how I was

feeling and I hadn't had that since mom left our home, she told me "if you carry a certain feeling spirit in your soul and body that would lead to an early death "I didn't know how to deal with the pain of being so silent and wanting to scream out and break down she told me the key to life is laughter try not to get emotionally angry or carry Bad feelings in your heart" I try to carry that with me in the back of my mind. after hours of conversation, I thanked the women and assured her that I was ok to leave and that I wouldn't do nothing stupid, that day I reflected to myself and realised that that was one of a few occasions where someone out of nowhere had saved my life because to be honest the way I was feeling I probably would of ended up making a stupid decisions based off my emotional sadness. And the mental torture that I was struggling to deal with that had built up inside me over a period. I never saw a doctor, or did I take prescription pills I just learned to heal myself by trying to let what I was going not define me.

Poetry

And there he was with eyes of love.
And thoughts that flow like streams
Alone inside a mind that's deep.
That grows through all his dreams.
A smile that hides a thousand wounds
A cry that no one hears.
And if they do it's usually late when
He's already wiped his tears.

– ElementOG

Now about my brother Ls –

My brother Ls is so much like me his caring with a good heart and soul he was 9 when I met him and from that moment we just got on from the start I was just excited to have a younger brother. Wow "your my brother come let me show you my room" he stood their with the sane kind of excited look on his face as me like he couldn't wait to see my room .. then from there on, everywhere I went he was with me, the park, at the shop, playing computer, playing football outside the front he was their "I love my brother" I use to say to myself at times His all about peace and love many times I been out with my brother and his refused to make me pay for something because he wants to pay for it that's the kind of person he is and I find I relate to him alot more because I'm similar in a sense of morals .. what I found as I grew from being around my brother now that we're grown adults was his level of maturity and how he stood on his own 2 when it came to making money or just dealing with his responsibilities and priorities he seemed like me to just know how to survive and stand as a man on his own 2 feet I never heard him ask, owe, beg, or borrow, and I respect that about him .. his a real one.

CHAPTER 8

FINDING MYSELF

I decided to do something that I felt was more in touch with where my skills and attributes lied and that was in sales marketing. My first working project was for a marketing company called (R.I.F. PROMOTIONS) my job description was going business to business selling merchandise and brokering deals. I really enjoyed it. it wasn't just the selling merchandise it was the structure of the business and how the formular of the business was set out we didn't just sell merchandise we would teach and train each other we had to go to a formular of 3 & 5 and 8 steps which was smile eye contact enthusiasm, which was quite simple if you smile ppl smile back eye contact gives ppl reassurance and enthusiasm means Ur excited about the product your selling because if you're not excited about Ur project then no one else will be. In the office I was responsible for training observations that was joining the company, the atmosphere was amazing, the average age group was between 18-25 .... there was a sense of friendly competition, but it made everyone just sell more merchandise and that meant making money which, after the office training we would transfer the information obtained from training into the field and try and do as many sales and marketing as possible. It wasn't just the sales that I enjoyed it was more the fact that there was so much opportunity for promotions and that is what gave me the drive and motivation to want to be a success. The formula was quite simple follow the simple steps go out in the field do 7 sales every day for 5 days for 2 weeks and you would be promoted as a trainee the would mean that you were promoted to trainee and now was able to train other colleagues and start to try and build Ur own team so how it would work was whoever the top 3 high rollers were a day they had the opportunity to take out observations which were other candidates that had successfully made it past the interview stage and wanted to join the company. so every day I would make sure that I was always focused, I was always in the office first before my team I felt like I had to start acting in the manager role to become one because eventually that's what I was trying to become if you managed to make it to trainee then your next steps was to try to become a crew manager which meant that you had to train 2 people in your team to be able to go out in the field following the 3,5,8, steps and successfully ring the bell or the hooter for 2 weeks and then you would be given a crew pin which now meant that you were capable of transferring the information onto others and leading by example and they were now able to generate money for the company not only that everything your team did the manager would give you a side cut from the overall profits if he could see that you had the potential which in my case the manager would sometimes take some of us high rollers out shopping while everyone else was in the field, so I bet your wondering what is the bell and the hooter. Well the bell and the hooter was something that was incorporated into the office to bring a buzz and excitement so basically if you came back from the field and you managed to do 7-9 sales then you would ring the bell if you did 10 or over then you would squeeze the hooter which was a bright orange horn but it got the office all vamped up and it brought a lot of fun and excitement amongst us, after a couple of weeks I was doing between 10-15 a day and we also had some other high rollers in the office when u came back to the office you would have to settle up Ur merchandise that you had not sold and brought back and settled up what funds you made for the company that day which was then split into % and you would get Ur cut to break it down simple we would sell pub restaurant cards for £20 and that would entitle you to 6 months' worth 2for1s and 10 coupons that you could use once each time on drinks which was a deal that was very successful. out of the £20 the company would take 1.5% and you would make the rest of the profit which would be £13 so there were days where you could leave the office with easy £200 a day depending on Ur work rate that's why I loved marketing because my manager at the time taught me that with sales and marketing you can own your own salary no one can tell you what Ur worth u create your own worth all you have to do is sell and that always stuck with me, after 18 months at the company I had hit many targets and broke many personal sales records and received many awards and accolades for my work and management skills we often did road trips to different offices the company had around the city and attended many award ceremonies, I remember attending an awards ceremony at the Wembley conference centre with the company it was called the rally I have no idea why they called it that but I guess my interpretation of it was that it was just because everyone from the company had been rallied together in one conference all the offices the company had around the city attended together to celebrate the achievements of others and to learn more about the company from some of the top executives and others that had been successful following the 3,5,8,steps everything was about the 3,5,8, steps I received rewards in plaques for my achievements and targets it was one of my proudest moments in my life, at the time it would of took a lot to top that as far as personal achievements, I remember I was sitting down In a row with my office and I was just overserving the show and I heard the category for highest sales in offices around the city and I remember they got to Birmingham and calling "Owen Williams "I was so shocked I turned to my manager and said "omg" he laughed and gave me a big hug and hand shake and said congratulations O you deserve it, the walk down the stage to collect my award that seemed forever my adrenaline was rushing I was so nervous but happy at the same time all my emotions were running around all at once. I finally made it to the stage and received my award I then made a short speech thanking everyone that had supported me and gave a special thanks to my manager that if it wasn't for him none of this would have been possible, he gave me a chance, he believed in me. had it not been for the company and my manager giving me this opportunity I would never have experienced so much I travelled from city to city and met so many people and learnt so much along the way it helped develop me as an adult and heled me grow in confidence especially when speaking to people, after I was in a comfortable position in the company the manager decided to rent a company house that wasn't far from the office that would accommodate 10 people I use to tell my manager that I had to catch to buses to work every day and it was all day and night sometimes starting at 9 and finishing at sometimes 9 so he asked me if I would like to rent a room which was covered by the company expenses, I took him up on his offer as it not only saved me money but it also meant that I didn't have to worry about not missing the last bus to get home I was in a house right near the office literally walking distance, not soon after the house was filled with 10 people from the office we all became really tight and close I saw it as a smart move from the manager because he had security that his high rollers were all living under one room cause we were making the company a lot of money, I appreciated his method and how he went about doing business I soaked up as much information as I could while I was around him as he wasn't always in the office he was always here one minute gone the next so most of the time he would ask one of me or the other crew managers to do the morning meeting which would require a motivational speech to get everyone ready to hit their targets, I would always go out with different teams everyday unless there was an observation and then I would take them lout week and work with them until they were in a position to make money on their own the thing with the job we were in was it was commission based so it meant that if you didn't do any sales then you didn't make any money, a lot of people came for observation and left the same day they found the commission based facts hard to accept as some came for money reasons and not the opportunity and saw the commission based situation as a pressure as some needed a regular guaranteed income I saw it as a challenge and a way of making as much as I could sell it was just my mind set and that what separated me from a lot others in the company, there were days where it was raining and I would be in the field and pass other colleagues in the pub and sitting in cafes waiting for the rain to stop, but they were the colleagues that had been in the business over 3 years and still only doing 2 to 3 sales a day and not going nowhere fast in the company. throughout the years at the company, I met so many people and interacted with so many top business associates but ...

CHAPTER 9

FIRST LOVE

Until now nothing compared to the one person I met that will always hold a special part in my heart she was half Korean and half Italian she joined the company and made a major impact almost instantly it was nice to have someone with her personality in the office and she was really good at the job she was actually given the fastest promotion in the company due to her hard work determination and natural ability to engage with others and was building a team that were Also really good, she had a good way with people and seemed to build a team quite easy because of her personality and the fact that she was beautiful her sole was what made her complete she was in touch with nature and was very intelligent and I loved that about her she taught me stuff that I never knew about myself and about life, about her search for success she had self-motivation and ambition, and she explained to me how education was top priority, I was amazed how she had come to this country on her own at 18 to further her education, for me it made me love and respect her more than anything. The fact that she was in another country with no parents new language new culture and she embraced it all really well I was well impressed by her story, we dated for a few years she taught me a bit of Italian and I show her how to cook jerk chicken and embrace my culture as much as I tried to embrace hers I did try to get the hand of using chop sticks I'd never tried using them before but I learnt how to use them after a while. After working together and living together for a few years the company went into liquidation the manager had moved office as he was going through some personal problems and had to move back to Australia we had some notice but it was a dramatic change for me as now we had to find somewhere to live and try to find another job, we decided to rent another property privately and tried to maintain but where we had moved to was right in the middle of the city on rotten park road which was at the time a known red light area I mean you couldn't even go to the shop after a certain time as the woman would literally think that I was there to pick up a client or something of that nature, as much as we needed a roof over our head things just started to take its toll and the area wasn't pleasant so we decided to rent a property more to where I was from it wasn't actually their but we moved to Stechford (manor road) and tried to make a home their I had a job working for an advertising company and she had found a job working sales too one day on my day off she had left as normal to go to work which required her catching the train to the city I was in bed still asleep until I was awaken to my phone constantly continuously bleeping none stop when I answered it she sounded really upset and shaken I told her to calm down and explain what was up she said that some guy had harassed and offended her at the train station and it wasn't the first time he had done so, it was just the first time she was telling me so with that I jumped up out my sleep and grabbed the first thing I could get my hands on which was a rolling pin out the kitchen draw I wasn't thinking because had I had been awake long and focused properly it wouldn't of been a rolling pin I would have been equipping myself with When I finally got to the train station I could see that she was upset which only made me more angry then she pointed out the guy that was harassing her for days I flew into a rage not knowing that before I had arrived police had already been called they must of arrived while I had my back to them because just as I approached the guy and went to strike him with the rolling pin police restrained me from behind I literally never even knew they were there I was arrested and things just went from bad to worse from there on I refused to be took into the van, back up was called the police eventually managed to restrain me and throw me in the back of the van and slammed the door behind them.

That same day I was released but I was charged with attempting to endanger a life and threatening behaviour of a civil servant I never knew that the guy was a civil servant he actually worked at the train station and was now considered an important part of the community and society just like policemen and women and bus drivers etc, I managed to still go to work as the bills needed paying but I was getting to the point in my life where I was losing my motivation day by day because I had this court case hanging over my head, for little moments work was keeping me focused and took my head out of the thoughts I was having if I was to sit at home all day doing nothing. eventually I had to attend court I remember attending Warrick crown court. just the building alone made you feel really weary about entering it, it had an old ancient look and feel about it like in the old days where prisoners were hung for hideous crimes, from the moment I approached inside the building everyone walking pass me just looked really important or seemed snobby or seemed like they thought I was guilty before I'd even saw a judge, I remember feeling well out my depth with the surroundings, I was put in a side room with my solicitor where I could have a chat about the possible outcomes and my pleas and just a run through how the process was going to work and what was going to take place attending the hearing, after my case being adjourned a few times I was finally up for sentencing where my solicitor told me that if I was to plead guilty I would only get a community discharge order for 12 months so it would mean that I would have to stay out of trouble for 12 months and not come before a judge in that duration of time or I would have to do the rest of the time I hadn't completed outside inside a prison, my initial plea was not guilty and I was happy to go to trial and fight my case but my solicitor somehow managed to talk me out of going to trial by explaining that if I was found guilty then I would be facing up to 2-4 years in prison, this made me second guess my initial decision and change my mind. I was finally called up next by the judge after I decided to plead guilty on the advice of my solicitor I remember standing in the dock looking behind me at my partner while she smiled with a reassuring look as none of the 2 of us was expecting the events what was about to occur in fact we had actually said just before I was called into the courtroom that we were going to go for food after this was over and go and have a little shop we actually didn't expect to be in their long literally thought I would get a 12 month conditional discharge order and then I could go for food and drinks and then go home but it was anything of that note. after feeling like id been standing for about an hour the judge finally made his decision, all I remember hearing him say was in a deep defiant stern voice "could you stand please this is a serious case and I take trying to inflict harm on another person as very serious not only that but a civil servant that I have no chose but to consider a sentence one of a custodial sentence" with that I turned around and I saw the look in my partners eyes but it was the solicitors face that told its own story she couldn't even look at me the judge told me to "turn around" and asked "are you listening and paying attention and do you understand what has just been said to you and what is about to take place" with that I replied with "yes" he told me to look at him he called my name and said that he had no choice but to sentenced me to 6 months in prison I couldn't believe what was going on it was all happening so fast I remember hearing my partner crying and in a low voice muttered the words "sorry this this is all my fault" but as I tried to answer her with "no its not "don't say that I'll be ok" I was escorted down the stairs with force.

I was slammed in a cell and left to gather my thoughts until the sweat box had arrived so I could be escorted to the nearest holding prison that had space, after falling asleep in the cell I was awoken to my cell door opening and the sound of "come on get yourself up on your feet the bus is here" that was the officer who was in charge of escorting all the prisoners that had been convicted that day onto the prison bus. I would ask the prison officer what jail I would be going to he replied with "ask no questions and you won't be disappointed Williams" he was very straight to the point I could see how he was liking the feeling of being empowered because I was cuffed and chained and literally vulnerable, I remember thinking to myself I bet you wouldn't feel so tough if I wasn't in here with cuffs on, as I gave him a side eye stare before I was finally escorted onto the sweat box, while I waited for other prisoners to fill the bus and then we were escorted from the court to Winson green the worst prison I could of actually been going too I had heard so much about this place heard so many stories and so much wrong doings so I knew I would have to get my mentality prepared to stand like a man and face whatever consequences along the way. as I started a 6 months sentence, all I could think about was how I had left my partner at the courtroom in tears and I didn't know how she was feeling but I knew she was blaming herself and that was really upsetting me knowing that she was on her own and she was also blaming herself for what I had endured it wasn't until I had actually made it onto the prison wing and spoke to the chapel that I finally managed to get a quick phone call I mean it was literally a quick phone call it felt like 10 seconds I said "hello are you ok try not to worry I be out soon it's not your fault ok I love you" she was upset I heard the officer shout to the chapel that that was enough time and that is when I realised reality hit home and I realised that this is going to be challenging because I wasn't one for taking orders and it wasn't that it was how you were given the orders and I didn't take kindly to how the orders were given out in prison. I had no control over my decisions I had no privacy no motivation no taste buds for the food and felt isolated. While in prison rumour had it that an officer called Mr S was alleged to have killed 2 inmates in the prison and he was not to be messed with and he was the officer on the spur I was on, he was about 6. 5 and was a loudmouth big bold head and took no crap from no one he was a real authorised figure.

I remember a day that always had kind of stuck with me, my pad mate at the time was like "just keep your head down and stay out the way" because he had already served time previously and had already experienced encounters with Mr S that wasn't pleasant, one day after I had had a shower on association and was making it back to my cell my name was called over the Tanoy by Mr S "Williams to the office" whenever you were wanted by member of staff you were called to the office over a Tanoy that echoed through the whole spur and landing I came to the office like yes guv Mr S just stood there for about 5 -10 seconds while he looked me up and down with an intimidating stare and said "shut the door behind you" he took out my file and went over it while I stood in silence "Williams" he said there are rules and regulations that I expect you to follow while you are hear like first tuck your shirt in and pull up Ur trousers there's women officers on the spur and I don't expect you to be dressing in that gang fashion, he carried on reading through my file and then said I'm going to make you B2 cleaner I never knew what that meant at the time so he ran through the job description and told me what was expected of me and what I would be paid weekly and that if I was caught on any other spur then I would get a nicking and lose my job, my job was quite simple after dinner any one that was a cleaner was let out the cells to clean their spur and sweep and mop the landings it got me out my cell so it was something that was good because it helped you get to know who was in the jail who was on your spur and it also got you known by everyone else because as soon as the cleaners were let out everyone else was banged behind their doors so other inmates would want you to keep passing and collecting parcels from different cells so they could cope while incarcerated I also but had to be smart about it because I had a tv in my cell and I was an enhanced prisoner so I didn't want to lose that because at the time it meant I was entitled to a visit a week and without being enhanced it was a visit a month and other little perks being an enhanced prisoner like going gym go library and being a cleaner I had a tv in my cell not all cells had a tv then they were just starting to build a new K wing that was going to have TVs in every cell and that was something that helped me to cope while serving time in prison having a tv was a time killer and I had a lot of that. I also was aloud my stereo that was sent in through an application system but again you needed to be an enhanced prisoner at the time to be able to obtain it, so I kept my head down most of the time but did do a few parcel passing for other inmates because I understood it was survival mode and that's just what it was while serving time I helped other inmates when I could and that's how I gained respect too because I was a B2 cleaner but I was one of the lads and even though I was in prison I never forgot where I came from it was always inmates against the system at all costs, I imagined myself behind my cell door and not being able to get access to paper pens smokes food and stuff so I helped out other inmates when I could like passing burn to cells passing magazines and biscuits and stuff it also helped me to form a bond with most of the other inmates that were on the same landing, I also did a bit of wheeling and dealing to get through my time I was receiving £15 at the time for my cleaning job I mean it's crazy that I would be getting up every day at 7pm until 7pm to clean landings for a wage of that amount I would never do such thing on the outside but this was just how much out of touch with reality being in prison is you literally have your civil rights taken well so it seemed. I would be awoken from the sound of my cell door banging with a metal object and lights flashing through Ur room you literally I had to be up and awake by the time the officer had made it round the whole prison landing spurs which had 3 landings with 40 doors on each spur. your bed had to be made blankets folded and then the officer who was working the spur would come back around and check your room was in an appropriate fashion to be scored A,B or C. if you got a C it would mean that you were banged up in your cell all day without being let out at all only for dinner while everyone else enjoyed association where you get your chance to have a shower use the phone and play pool and mingle with other inmates for a couple of hours or until it kicked off and everyone was put back behind their cell door, in my time in prison I seen so many things that I wouldn't have believed had I not saw them myself I saw people cut up really bad and having to be moved off the wing I witnessed inmates being hot watered and sugared which was a daunting experience I quickly learnt how to make a lighter in prison using tissue a shank using my toothbrush and a razor blade I saw inmates make jewellery boxes out of matchsticks which was amazing and I came across some absolute excellent drawers of art with a pencil, not all people in prison were actually bad people I quickly understood that some peoples situations were just unavoidable and others was just silly decision making but not all people in prison were people with bad intentions. I had older wiser men tell me to try my best not to come back here because prison just stops your growth in life, and everything will continue to develop and change around you. I took it as a metaphoric way of them saying the world doesn't revolve around you or anyone else at that matter and will continue regardless, also I met a lot of intelligent inmates real smart people with degrees and businesses. I was finally released in 1999 and the love of my life and I decided to still be friends but to go our separate ways we both sat and amicably decided it was the best thing as she had received a job offer that was far away and she decided to take it and no way was I going to stand in her way as she was very talented and ambitious. there was a part of me that was broken but I knew it was for the best. That was the first time that I had ever experienced having my heart completely broken all I know is that I didn't like the feeling and I was never planning on feeling like this ever again.

Chapter 10

Through A Writer's Eyes

While my time in prison I spent most of my time writing lyrics and basically just expressing how I was feeling at the time I found it easier at the time to write my thoughts on paper on release I came home with a book full of rhymes and an afro and couldn't wait to have a nice soak in a home bath. I managed to keep my flat that I had prior to going to prison in (whitebeam road chelmsley wood) because I had only been in prison 3 months, I had my brother keep an eye on my bills and flat, so the housing wasn't aware I was away for long, so I was thankful to him for managing to keep my 1-bedroom flat. I spent a lot of time at home writing and rapping continuing to perfect my craft I fell in love with writing it helped me to self-counsel myself and get a lot of things off my chest and in my mind, and it was what I wanted to do. not only did I have self-motivation I developed a passion for writing plus with my idol being 2pac I felt like that was the extra bit of inspiration I needed whenever I felt like giving up because honestly I don't think I could of got through some of the experiences I endured without 2pacs music I felt like I related to his struggles, I started looking for music studios around the centre of Birmingham town as there wasn't much facilities offered in my county where I lived so I would spend hours scouting studios and just having a look around to see which studio I was feeling a vibe in. I came across a project called muzik links it was set up to help young talented youth nurture their talents, I met the founder and he introduced me to everyone in the project while I was getting to know everyone I got to know and young youth similar to myself he was also talented and ambitious and felt like he had a lot to offer but he didn't write music or rap he produced beats he was talented he so we spent hours and hours kicking it and chilling and learning and he invited me to his studio that he had set up not too far from the project that we were both attending at the time from their I never looked back I spent hours, days in the studio he understood my style and he encouraged me that I was hot "you rap different to these other guys" he said "I feel your pain" he made the beats and I rapped it was a match up that was hard not to recognise at the time after perfecting my style and craft I started working on a mix tape so I could put something out for the streets I did 14 tracks and I called my first mixtape through a writers eyes "my producer encouraged the title because he always said to me "O" you're not just a rapper your different you are an artist, a writer" it's one of the things that helped me to keep writing because he would always tell me that I was sick or one of the best out in Birmingham so that helped a lot with feeling confident to release music to the streets, at times I felt the words my idol had said in a song I'm just a young black male that felt like I had been cursed since birth" but somewhere inside me was that inner belief that I could make it to achieve something or be someone in life and not just stand for nothing, I was determined.

While in between the studio going back and forth I came across a lot of other rappers that were also inspired to make it in the music industry...There were so many groups flying the flag for Birmingham at the time just a few to mention. (Tiny presents) (B6 slash) (Blood Brothers) (Shadowless) along with other up and coming rappers that were hungry waiting for their chance! Birmingham was the place If you were looking for real homegrown creative hardcore rappers! I met some people with alternative motive but also met some good people come to mind is a cool dude called (giz) he had his own group called (Royalist mud gully) and they were mostly brothers like myself and I kind of related to him, overall I think it was a spiritual connection he moved a certain way and always shown me and my team respect anytime I was around him he was like a humble boss in his establishment and I respected his movement and like me he wanted his team to win him and his team could spit rap they were considered at the time in my eyes the hardest out, to me they were the group that were the closest competition in my eyes but it was in a respectful way and they had a lot of street respect at the time and so did we so it was only inevitable that we did collaborations on various tracks that still go down now as an underground street classic, we always invited them onto our shows and whenever we were kicking it in the studio they would come through with their whole team and it was always love them man were like family from another family most weekends we would be played all over pirate radio we would sit and wait for our song to be played it gave us confidence that the streets were listening and the feedback was always positive thanks to hot 92 sting FM, DJ mega stress, miss banks and noodles and banky these were the hottest pirate radio stations at the time, but gratefully I met all these guys through a man called "P walker" who at first I thought had other intentions with our music but he turned out to be a good guy he helped to grow my buzz and I will always be grateful because he did a lot for the underground streets for those, with his radio station plus he hooked me up with some producers that were really good too, we got a good buzz to the point where people were actually requesting our songs, I did performances all over the city London, Manchester, Bristol, piccadilly square, Nottingham and Birmingham academy and alexander theatre thanks to a man called big cipher he was someone that I had a lot of respect for and he helped navigate me through the industry he had the biggest group in Birmingham they had the most sales in the street as far as numbers and his group were known more on a global stage I respected him highly and his team (MD7) they put Birmingham on the map in fact they were the first group that I heard rapping for the UK so they will always go down as a massive influence in the UK rap scene they were made up of 3 dudes I had a lot of respect for I didn't really know the 3rd member but anytime I saw him we always shown mutual respect and I know he helped a lot of the youth from around the inner cities and was doing positive things but the other member was a dude called (Malik) we chopped it up more and had a little bit more of a music relationship for me respectively he had the best flow out the 3 and he could really spit he was nice with the word play and the flow it was more than an honour to have collaborated with him on a track ft big cipher I was grateful for the opportunity because it helped grow my rap reputation but (big Cipher) was the man who pulled all the stings behind the scenes and he inspired me and he was a very humble man whenever I needed some advice and guidance I felt like he was someone I could trust he even encouraged me to attend a music business course that he was running to help people understand the business side of things and get a better understanding of the business side of the music industry and I will always be grateful for that. I decided to put together my own showcases and the first showcase I put together was at the medicine bar Digbeth I never had a lot of support and sponsors but I appreciated (mark Dwayne) he was a grafter "I literally watched mark single handedly grow his business from the ground up" I would see Mark out everyday on the ramp! I would see mark out every day on the ramp in Birmingham promoting his brand he was passionate and I learned a lot just from the way he approached people also another dude who I respected for his hustle called was (krazer) I use to see him out selling his own CDs and I respected that about him the fact that he was up grinding away selling CDs at 3 pound a pop just like me how could I not respect that, but (mark Dwayne) he single handedly put together his own magazine and his street cred magazine team covered the whole event and that only made me and my group (5th Element) more popular more marketable and gained a lot more respect, because at the time the street cred was one of the biggest magazines in Birmingham as far as covering positive things and amazing things to do with the black culture and positive things that happened in the city so it was a good look for me and them but overall put 5th Element was the new name in the Birmingham rap game, I put the show together myself and it was a really good successful show, the aim was to get every rapper /artist from every part of the city together and showcase our talents and skills network and have some unity.

Another man that I looked up to in the music game was a dude by the name of dada diamond I met him through my older cousin D he was a righteous dude he had his own swagger his own style but through his music I respected him and had saw him putting in a lot of work, he had a good style and was a real good dude he would always tell me that he rates my music and my words and what I stand for, I later on found out he was a July born dude like myself always preaching positivity to me anytime we had a chance to sit and chop it up we did many collaborations together on songs I really felt his music so it was only right that we would feature on many songs together but he was another dude that I gained respect for from the music game in fact I had many music videos with dada diamond and every time I've worked with him was always a pleasure I learnt a lot off him he was very knowledgeable on deep topics that sometimes I had no idea about but I would try and soak up what information I could anytime I would chop it up with him but ultimately he was someone who I had a lot of time for. further to that my life was in a bit of a spiral because I was going studio but needed money to fund everything plus I was now in a one bedroom flat I had bills and benefits wasn't cutting it and I was finding it very hard to get a job after numerous no responses and no thankyous to my job applications I started feeling the pressure and then that quickly turned to frustration and pressures of life crept in and so I turned to the only way I knew of survival and that was selling drugs (not to glorify) but I started off just moving a little bit of cannabis but I smoked weed and I wasn't really seeing the kind of profit that I was expecting, I would say I was smoking £20 a day and plus I had friends and bothers that smoked at the time and they would most of the time want something for free so I wasn't really profiting because I would literally give it out for free so it wasn't long before I was selling everything that made a profit weed crack cocaine and heroin at the time I never realised the detrimental effects that this kind of drug did to my community I only thought about the money I was making and it was good I was making anything between £500 –1000 a week I was paying y own bills and living quite good I brought a car had my own place and had money to put away I was feeling like a man, at the time I never realised but the game I was in was a business I was a kind of business man but just not legally but I never looked at it like that at the time I would say I was naive and reckless my car I was driving was insured and taxed but I never had a legal license so on many occasions I had to evade police I use to do business with my pal M's. My (brother T) (Yardz) and my cuz (Rhino). Now just to tell you a bit about my cousin rhino, he was my cousin on my dads side so my dads sisters son he was about 6"6 and was built like a rhino! Was quiet and humble loved laughing and was always giving us stories from stuff he knew or stuff he did he would give us jokes one thing he could do was drive he loved cars he hooked me up a few times when I was buying cars he had good links we did good business, he was from B6 part of town but was always over my neck if the woods in the year 2000's he also had his own runnings with the law Robbery's for substantial amounts and other minor offences which is all documented we were close he would always hang out and kick it with me in the studio at my house on the street we spent a significant amount of time around each other! Before I was locked up I remember a time that came to my head with rhino where it was about 2am and I was asleep earlier that day I had yardz rhino and a few overs over my house I hadn't realised who had stayed and who had left but all I remember was a loud bang on my door "armed police everyone stand still nobody move" they had came to raid my property on suspicion of fire arms and drugs because of the shock of it all and so many guns pointing at my head a chest they asked me as they came bursting through my bedroom door "how many people are in the property" I said just me and my friend is on the sofa I never knew that no only yardz was on the sofa but rhino had stopped over also so while me and yardz were being cuffed I heard "freeze theirs another one" to my amazement they almost shot rhino out of fright as they never knew he must of been asleep on the other sofa covered with a blanket and as it was dark and all I could see was flashing lights and loud shouting! Eventually we were all apprehended and taken to the station where I took full responsibility for the evidence that was shown to me which was a prop hand gun that could of been converted to a real gun they said and some weed which was enough for personal use .. I was later bailed until a later date where I was eventually only charged with possession of cannabis but do you know that still to this day that I have possession of firearms on my record and can't be approached by one police officer on their own, I don't know if that's a good thing or a bad thing to be honest it's not something that I like! Because it's the kind of thing that stays with you and don't allow you to grow as a person and can also ruin opportunities in work and in life! But all that done was make me a target whenever I would step outside as we were all on the police radar in some kind of way, plus with what I was doing in was only a matter of time before I would be repenting for my actions.

CHAPTER 11

HUSTLING BACKWARDS

I started seeing my good friend Blanco's sister at the time, and she was aware of what my occupation was she also was a bit of a hustler so we hit it off quite naturally, she was also doing her own ones and twos and I had already knew who she was as it was my friends sister and I had previously had brief conversations with her whenever I would see her at his house. as we were now a couple we decided that we would hustle together I don't know who actually suggested it but we put some money together and started doing what we had to do to survive because she also had come from a survival situation in life too, we both had the same birthday which was funny to we took holidays had fun brought a lot of material things and just kind of lived it up you could say in between being in the streets I would be back and forth to the studio so I was always on the move there were times where I would get a call for a sale and when I would go to do the drop there would be 3 and 4 people in the phone box and police not too far coming around at the corner, it was almost like a cat and mouse game with the police because I k new they knew what I was up to but I also know that they had to catch me and I wasn't going to let them do that, then in an afternoon of madness after I had just booked a holiday and feeling like I just wanted to get away for a while and just have a chill because it was no use making all this money and not actually doing anything with it and I liked travelling was something I liked doing I wanted to see some of the world and go and embrace the cultures, that day I just felt like chilling and relax until the holiday date it was only a couple of days to wait so I didn't feel like I wanted to do any kind of business I don't know what it was just had this weird feeling that was over me that was trying to get me to just chill but my partner at the time had come home and said she was going to pick something up, I remember saying to her "nah I isn't getting nothing I just want to chill we should just kick back until we come back from holiday but she was showing me how the phone was ringing off and we loosing sales and money so she was determined to get something no matter what I said before she left I gave her some money to get me something small and she left I remember her answering a call and saying" yeh picking it up in 20 mins "I shook my head and continued my day I remember all day that day I just didn't feel right I had a weird feeling inside it wasn't until later on that night that that feeling was about to make sense, one night after I had finished doing a few sales and writing I locked up as usual and went to bed as my partner was stopping over that night all of the drugs that was brought that day was all inside my house then out of nowhere there was a bang on the door "police open up" police open up bang "bang bang" I jumped up from the sounds of the windows on my door being put through. I got to the door and they asked me to open the door but with all the shouting and screaming and noise from the smashed glass I panicked and quickly ran back in the room and asked my partner where the stuff was and at this time we were both fing and blinding finally the police managed to gain entry to my house and came into the bedroom and told us both to stand still and don't move I was cuffed and asked if there is anything illegal in the property I never replied and me and my partner were separated into separate parts of the house while the police carried out their raid. after about what seemed a lifetime the police finally finished their raid and brought the items contained from the search into me and asked me if I knew what this was. "no comment" with that I was arrested for possession with intent to supply also money was obtained scales and a couple ounces of cannabis that was sitting on my living room table, you didn't even need to open the bag you could smell the cannabis it was that strong, after being lead out the property I could see all the damage the police had done to not only the door on my property but the inside of it, every cupboard had been pulled out in every room they left my house an absolute mess.

While being escorted to the police van I noticed my neighbours were either at the window or outside the door looking on nosey at all the commotion, I remember feeling a bit embarrassed and just being led away by police in hand cuffs and all the commotion made it seem like I committed a murder but never the less from an observers point of view you could see it was something serious I had done, while down the station I was made to wait for my solicitor until I was questioned about the various findings "do you know what this is" "no comment I said looking at the bag containing what appeared to be crack cocaine" I'm showing the p,i,c another bag containing heroine I again said no comment I was then shown various other objects like scales and money I answered no comment all the way and was charged with possession with intent to supply and had to go to court the following day to answer bail conditions. After I was finally released and went home, I was met with all the mess the police had left in my house I remember pushing the door open it wasn't even locked my place had been ransacked after spending hours tiding up I finally got the place back to some sort of normality and then reflected on the events that had taken place that morning, I was trying to hold it together while my partner was panicking, "were going to go to prison" "I can't believe it what are we going to do" I told calm her down and tried to reassure her not to worry and said that I would sort it and not to worry but deep inside I knew what she was saying was kind of true but I never shown her that I was worried because one of us needed to be the strong one, previous to what had happened I had already booked a holiday to Greece so the day had come where I was supposed to be enjoying a nice break away, the situation took something away from the excitement of going away on holiday but the holiday came at the right time to just get away from everything for a week, after enjoying a week away I was finally back to face the music of the court case regarding being charged with possession with intent to supply, it was a serious charge deep inside my heart I knew that it would contain a custodial sentence, and just never knew exactly how much time I would be serving. while waiting to be called up by the judge my solicitor took me my partner and her brother

Blanco that had also been arrested as he was found in my partners property with an undisclosed amount of cannabis on the same day, my solicitor said "this is what the deal is you can both go guilty or going not guilty and being found guilty your looking at 6-8 years with that my partner started panicking and threating so I sat and made a conscious decisions and I decided that I was going to take the ownership of everything and not only that it got my partner off and she was able to have a life outside and not be affected by the situation plus I loved her at the time and I was the man and I didn't want her to go to prison so I stood up and took the fall for everything like a man should so that she could walk free, sitting and pondering the situation for a while the judge finally called me to the dock I remember thinking "let's just get this over and done with" I was mentally prepared, my friend Ian B had wrote a letter for me to give to the judge explaining that I was sorry for my actions and I had remorse he told me that I had to think smart and that the judge would look at that as some kind of accepting responsibility and that it would be taken into a positive consideration when sentencing, I will always be grateful for what he did for me the letter was perfect, my friend Ian B, was brilliant at writing things like this and it really helped because I don't think I could of put together what he did and how he wrote it in the amount of time I had, after what seemed like a long telling off which was actually a briefing from the judge I was told to stand, "I have read your letter one of remorse and I have taken into consideration your early plea of guilty so I'm going to sentence you to 3yr 5months I was quickly took away before I could say my goodbyes and took to the waiting cells until the bus was ready to escort me to a prison, I remember thinking to myself that all the people I had helped out all the favours I did for people all the times I sorted out situations for people and not one of those people was in the courtroom when I was being sentenced except my homeboy Ian B, who never once asked me for a favour or a dime (now that's real) I didn't even know what to think but I knew one thing and that was that I had been here before previous to the assault and thief conviction, so I was much more mentally prepared this time. when the sweat box finally arrived the officer said that we were going to Redditch which was hmp hewell at the time I had never been here so I didn't know what to expect regarding the prison itself like the rules and regulations, while on the wing I was put into a cell with a guy called Robot he was standing outside his cell when I arrived refusing to have anyone else share his cell as there was only 5 new inmates that had arrived with me that day for him to choose from, "right in there you go then" said the officer who had escorted me to the cell he told robot he was putting my match in with him because he was loud but I looked and said "guv Ur funny I'm chilling I'm here to do my time and get the hell out of here all these other games and matches and stuff you do you can do that with some of the other inmates" guv said "oh we got a smart mouth haven't we" we got to watch you" with that I walked into the cell room and left guv outside the door "left side is yours" robot said and try to take a shit while you're on association so we don't have to use the toilet in the room, that was one of the rules that was fine with me, after weeks of being in the prison my cousin Marcus had also been transferred to the wing and was head servery as he was doing a long sentence he was almost coming to an end of his time "yoo cuz you good" "yooo omg yessss family" I replied with a big embracing hug "Yeh man just here they got man caged down but all good, you know what it is" every day he would come to my cell and chill and he would send stuff down to my cell to make sure I was blessed and always sorted plus as he was on servery he always patterned up my dinners that was until I was transferred to hmp Featherstone.

When I arrived there it was a cat c prison so it was a bit more less risk and more activities I played football against the other officers and went to the gym a lot whenever there was a spare slot, anytime I was in my cell I would concentrate more and more on writing continuing to release all the thoughts that I had on my mind onto paper I wrote track after track I then entered the prison church band it was cool I would write music with the band from the church and it was really refreshing and it took my mind of actually thinking of being in prison while I was there, at this point I could only take day by day I realised that there's no mercy in this world especially on the streets I remember reasoning with myself thinking nobody can help me make my dreams come true you can only achieve what you desire and I really saw myself as a talented artist and I was determined to spend my time writing as much as I could. while I was serving time in prison me and the band did live music performance for the prison like a music performance in prison and I really enjoyed it I loved music it took me to a place where nothing or no one else could take me, I wanted to write and rap about the harsh realities of the streets the society and how it affected me the dangerous elements in the inner cities and the things that went on in my environment, writing was a way also for people to hear what I had to say I felt like writing gave me a voice, I tried to research as much information as possible from books in the library about various successful people. one thing that stood out to me was the way that most people I read about had faced some kind of adversity before they made it to be a success, I never read so much until I came to prison, in fact I don't think I actually read a full book besides when I was in school but it just came back to me naturally, I remember one day I was sitting on my bed in my cell and it was mail time I saw that the officer had put a few envelopes under my door one was for my pad mate and the other 2 were for me the officer at the time because my cell mate had to sign for something because he had to sign for a postal order I noticed the officer looking at me with a smirk on his face which I felt was quite weird but I never took it as nothing at the time "you alright Williams" he said I said "yep I'm good guv" after my cell mate had signed he closed the door and I sat on my bed ready to open my mail I use to open my letters and always read the end first it was just something I did so I turned my letter and it read the following "you be strong, I'm not as strong as you" "I can't do this no more take care I'm sorry" I couldn't believe what I was reading, I read it again as tears started to fill up my eyes I looked away as I didn't want my cellmate to notice me and I turned the letter around and read it from the start to finish about 10 to 20 times I just couldn't take it in what I was reading eventually I couldn't hold the emotion together and my cell mate noticed I was down he try to tell me to forget that chick and I can't afford to let that be my focus or I won't survive in here but it was easier said than done, when I finally got myself together that day I sat and realised the officer that was smirking at me when he opened the door at and asking me if I was alright must have read my mail before he gave it me and saw that I was being dear john! Dear john is a term used in prison when you receive a letter from your partner saying she is leaving you" he must of got some sort of kick out of it but I got myself together with the help of reading books and writing music about what I was going through, I became obsessed with reading peoples stories that was like no others, what I drawn from them was belief if not anything else and never to give in or give up and that I could achieve whatever I put my mind too.

Featherstone was quite a big prison I was on the drug free wing and decided that to try to spend some of my time educating myself, I did my gcse's in prison English, maths, personal development and I got a lot better at using a computer (pc) I remember receiving my certificates and they came in the form of Manchester college they looked well-presented which had (ocr) written on the front in big letters so it was official like you couldn't tell that I had studied in prison it was set up that way to help other inmates that wanted to study the chance to still get some sort of education so they could put themselves in a better position on release. I enjoyed studying plus it got you out your cell, and it was what was keeping me focused and helped me to cope in a big way, everyone did their time differently in prison you just had to leave everyone to it but I could never get my head around inmates that woke up and crossed off a number off their release date calendar list, I always thought that was torture and would just drag my sentence out longer, especially if you had to do over 2,000 days I mean imagine sitting there waking up thinking "oh well only 1,999 days to go" I think that would of affected my mental state and drove me insane, for me staying busy was the way, most inmates were from Wolverhampton or Birmingham I managed to get myself a drug support worker counselling job which required helping other inmates that was experiencing difficulty coping in prison as it being their first time inside I remember my first time in prison and I did have anxiety and all sorts of emotions running through my body so I could kind of relate to some of the first timers situations so my s/o put me forward for the position, in between that I had to sit little tests that made the prison aware that I had an understanding of the role, it was refreshing actually helping others and it passed my time and it also looked good on my record for whenever I was going to be considered for my cat D release, I played dominos with some of the older inmates and occasionally the odd game of pool but most of the time I was either on the phone or writing some poetry or music in my cell. I entered a few gym competitions and got a little reputation for my physique I was in good shape I always had been prior to coming to prison all prison did was allow me to build on my physique that I had already and make me stronger because I was already chiselled. I finally got my cat D and was quite excited at the prospect of being able to go home every 28 days for 3-5 days leading up to my release from prison first I had to do 3 months in the prison then I would be considered home leave where I would be able to go home for 3 whole days and return back to the prison for another 28 days and then you would be allowed home for 5 days after that and every time until release when I arrived at hmp hewell I never knew what to expect I remember pulling up in the bus and just seeing one big massive house it looked like an old mansion that had been forgotten about, on arrival with the other inmates I couldn't wait to just get in and do my first 3 months so I could start going home, this was nothing like a prison the rooms was made up of dorms so there were anything form 5-10 man dorm I was in a 10 man dorm it was alright id never experienced nothing like it before but I got along with it everyone was quite cool and as long as no one was invading my space or caught stealing out my belongings then I was ok with it I had access to the kitchen I could cook my own breakfast and lunch I had a lot more freedom and really didn't feel like I was in prison I could even walk out onto the field and actually see normal civilians using the foot path for jogging or walking their dogs, I never could understand why some inmates would escape and run off when they were almost going home because the officers would never chase you they would let you go and within 2-3 days you were normally picked back up and that would ruin any chance of being able to go home and see family and friends you would be put back into a closed cat B jail where your security risk would now be a concern so the chances of being considered for cat D in the future would mean other requirements would need to be met and I wasn't trying to end up in that situation as it had took me over a year to get here. After completing 3 months I was now being considered for my first 3 day home leave I was so excited I just couldn't wait to just get out even if it was just for a minute whether being released on day released or home leave the prison policy was that I had to have someone of support sign me out and pick me up so my brother ls's use to sign me out for my home leaves on my leave my brother had mentioned that a girl mentioning how she had saw pictures of me in jail and thought I was looking good and that she wanted to send me some photos I finally got in contact with her and we arrange to meet on my next home leave the next time I was due to come out, and she agreed. Whilst being in hmp Hewell I was able to make my own breakfast I was making boiled eggs and porridge and literally whatever I wanted it, it was far from any other kind of prison I had ever been to. On my next home leave I was able to obtain the keys from my brother for his one bed bedsit that he had in Stechford where I spent some time with miss L and a laugh we chilled and watched movies she had a thing for Haribo's and sour sweets so I made sure that I stacked her up with s few packets after spending most of the day together I was picked up from my brother and I after dropping miss L back to her home I went to visit family and friends, even though I was out on home leave I wasn't able to smoke cannabis as I would be drug tested whenever I would return back to h.m.p Hewell so whenever I was around family I would have to be very discipline because most of them smoked cannabis, one day I was on my way back to the Hewell after a nice 5 day home leave and I had some cannabis on me that I contemplated taking back in to Hewell with me so I could have a sessions with the lads I told my brother and I remember him telling me that it wasn't a good idea but I said "its ok they don't really search you in here bro they won't suspect anything" but that day when I returned back the governor was on and the head s/o so all officers was doing things by the book with strict intentions "stirp search Williams the officer said" I hesitated and quickly threw the cannabis that I managed to get into my hand into a plant pot that was situated by the door entrance as I entered the main room to be searched I went through as normal not thinking that the officer had suspected anything, I went to my dorm and continued my day as usual letting everyone in my dorm know what my home leave was like and how much I never wanted to come back. a couple of days went by and out of nowhere while I was with some inmates in the dorm getting ready to go to the kitchen a few officers were walking in my direction towards my dorm "Williams" I heard one of the officers say "pack your stuff and come with us" I asked the officer why was I being escorted and they told me that I would be told once I packed my stuff and made my way to the office. Once I finally made my way to the office I was explained to that the officer that searched me on the way back from my 5 day home leave had his suspicions and checked the cctv and noticed that I had hid some cannabis in a plant pot outside the main door, I shook my head but didn't respond verbally I couldn't believe I could be so stupid that I had just ruined any chance of going home every 28 days, I was now being escorted back to lock up back in a cat B jail to finish my last 8 months before I was released.

Initially I felt like a wounded animal to think one minute I was going home and seeing family and friends and able to just feel free have sex have fun and just do all the things that I had missed while being incarcerated and the next minute all of them incentives and privileges had been lost from making one silly decision. When the prison van arrived I was escorted into the van and remember sitting in the van feeling like I had been travelling for hours until eventually the van finally came to a slowing down and then a standstill, "(h.m.p) alter course" the officer said "only one to get rid of" I looked at the officer like you got some cheek shook my head and realised I only had myself to blame I was back in a lock up prison but it was a private prison and it was run completely different, it was run different in a sense of it was a semi open jail you didn't have as much free roaming as (h m p) Hewell but you wasn't locked up all day either you were out your cell 7 till 8 and it was situated different you literally had 3 landings and it was mixed with y/o's but they were on the 1's landing separated from the older inmates I was mixing with youths and adults from Birmingham but mostly Toxteth lads. there was a lot of opportunity for education, and I took it up. I was put on servery because the officers were sick of inmates bullying servery lads for extra food and wanted someone put on servery that couldn't be pushed about, I was 13 stone at this stage and most of my body was pure muscle I was never someone that carried much body fat it was just how my body metabolism was. Once I was settled into (h.m.p) alter course I received notification that my phone numbers that I had been waiting to be transferred onto my pin had all been checked out and cleared and I could now use the phone. I phoned miss L to let her know what had happened that I had been transferred back to lock up prison in Liverpool and she said she wanted to come and see me I advised her not to as I was phoning to let her know that I was ok and that I would no longer be coming home on home leaves "no way" she said "you are kidding me aren't you" I told her I was being serious and after a couple of minutes she realised I was being serious by the tone I was using in my voice, "are you alright" she said I need to talk to you about something I said "what's up is everything ok" she said "yeh I'm pregnant "I was in shock I was like "what you kidding me" I think she thought I was going to be upset about it but I was over the moon I was having my first child I remember feeling over joyed for a minute but then had to remember I was in prison, she said "are you happy" I replied with hell yeh I was laughing and joking with, miss L on the phone until finally my phone credit started bleeping so I had to hang up "see you soon I said rest up and chill until I'm released and take it easy ok" "ok" she said "bye "with a little giggle before the credit went. I started preparing, myself for life on the outside and now I had to think about having a child, my first child I remember thinking to myself "thank you lord thank you" I'm going to be a dad. While in my cell it was coming close to being banged up and I could see an officer walking towards my cell with some papers in her hand "Williams" she said "these are for you" I took the papers and had a look and to my amazement it was my release papers for tag I was shocked as I had not applied for tag but what had happened was miss L had phoned up my probation and notified them that we were having a baby and that I would have suitable accommodation for tag because a monitor sensor had to be fitted into her premises to be able to keep a track of my movements with an electronic device around my ankle, I agreed and signed the papers and gave them back to the officer, the officer had a brief conversation she said "Williams you're a good lad you got a chance to change your life and do the right thing when your released don't ever come back here" I made a joke and said "well what if I want to come and see you" she nudged me on my arm and said "I'm being serious your better than this place plus you have a son on the way so try and put all your focus into getting a job and providing for your son and set a good example to him" I had done many courses "from" the effects of drugs, to peer pressure, to personal development, to substance misuse, to accountability, but the course I took the most from was victim awareness because I was sentenced for supplying drugs, I opted to do a victim awareness course so I could get an understanding of who is affected by the misuse of drugs it was to show that I now had a full understanding of my charge and that I was remorseful in some way, it wasn't until the course started that I was informed that we would have victims from the outside come and take part and share their stories of how and when they had been victims and how it affected them, I remember an old lady speaking to me about being affected by her son being a drug user but she was affected by him stealing and drug dealers threating her for money her son had owed and also been attacked mugged and beat up for money as little as £5 pound it really touched my heart I had Read so many stories about things like this happening but never heard stories first hand from actual victims like I did that day, It touched my heart in a different way I told the lady that I now have a full and better understanding of myself and how she had helped open my mind to think of how my actions affects others, being a drug dealer like I was has affected so many but at the time I only thought about the money I was young and naive and reckless but that was no excuse.

I remember going back to my cell after that day and really over thinking about what the lady had told me my brain was scrambled I couldn't get out my head that there were scumbags out there that actually beat up old ladies for valuables or money and it was all for the love of drugs, and prior to this I felt responsible as I was a dealer so I vouched to myself that I would never consider going down that path again. I think I needed to do the victim awareness course it made me reflect so much and take accountability of myself and my actions I self-reflected a lot on my past self I realised that if I was going to change then I would have to change the way that I saw the world and try to change the way that I saw myself more important and to think about the choices I was going to make and about the things that were most important in my life, while serving my time in prison I tried to read as much books as possible I read a book by Einstein and something that always stayed in my mind was !that "we cannot solve our problems with the same thinking we used to create them" so I knew I had to change the way that I was thinking, I spent time being self-aware and analytical about how I looked at myself and the things that were not good for me I was a lot less disorganised and unpredictable and I had to tell myself who do I need to become in order to hit the targets and goals that I had set for myself, many times I had honest conversations with myself pending my release. I realised that I projected a lot of my hurt and insecurities upon others and I had to change that I had to take responsibility of myself.

CHAPTER 12

BIRTH OF MY SON
AND DAUGHTER

I was finally released 2.2.2010. and tagged to miss L premises. She had already had 3 kids previous from other relationship and was pregnant with my son who was due to be born any time soon in fact I was released 1 month before my son was born, the day at the hospital was a mad experience we had been their 10 hours while miss L was in labour then finally I heard "push" "push come on keep going" I was next to miss L holding her hand for comfort as she took a deep breathe "come on your doing well you can do it you're doing well" she looked at me with them "shut the hell up eyes" but she was also emotional and full of screams and tears finally my son was born 5 weeks premature he was so small immediately the midwife and nurse got some scissors and gave them to me and I cut the cord. Could you turn the music off the nurse said as I had had on unborn child by 2pac playing right as my son was being born that was also a magical moment it just happened that way, I hit the pause button and apologised with a smile and the nurse said "its ok I understand but we must be mindful of others in the facility" finally I got to hold my son I started crying with joy tears and emotion "I love you son" I love you" I said as I cuddled him in the towel he was wrapped it in my arms, I then gave him to miss L and she said "I love you son you're so small" we both had a teary few moments before the nurse came to do the necessary checks on miss L and my son "aww his so cute the midwife said" then they drew the curtain and carried out a few extra checks on his heartbeat his lungs and his hearing it was all precaution but a little extra because my son was born 5 weeks earlier than he was actually due to be born, finally we got him home and spent our first night home with our son, couple of months in and things got a little stressful miss L had 3 other kids and everything seem to get a little manic at times but we coped as best as she could plus as I was only there a couple of days a week to see my son after, my tag had run out because if I was registered to be living at the property it would of effected miss L benefits and housing benefits so I got myself a job and was stopping at my uncles B house in between that's why I always have a different kind of love for my uncle B, because he was always there for me no matter what it was if it was just to talk or offer advice and support he took time to understand me, 1 year later impact on 19.08.2011 when miss L had just finished eating a curry she had told me that she didn't feel any contractions then out of nowhere like literally out of nowhere she phoned me and was screaming in agony immediately she was escorted to the hospital but it was different to the one the our son was born in the after all the pushing and screaming and gas and air miss L finally gave birth to a beautiful perfect baby girl, she was like a little princess and she was everything that we both wanted she was perfect she came at a time where I was in a good space she was really small had loads of hair and a nice healthy set of lungs with her screams, I remember holding her first, I stroked her face and kissed her gently miss L was crying with joy "I love her" she's a princess she's perfect she looks like you o", I told her the opposite I said "she looks like a miniature you" with a smile on my face with that she managed to try a little smile as she also was in pain and understandably so from the experience of giving birth to our daughter, "it's alright for you isn't it" she said I pretended I didn't hear her and said you did well you did really well I cut the cord and then handed our princess to miss L she was so happy and emotional and I was too, after our daughter was settled miss L had to go time to have a rest after the ordeal she had been through I went to go and I left the hospital to go and get my brother and my son, on my way back to the hospital an altercation had started between miss L and one of the ward nurses and miss L wanted to leave I was like "err what's going on "the next thing I know she's storming off with our daughter and the nurse as alerted security as miss L had not allowed the nurse to finish our daughters hearing test which is their procedure before they can give a baby the all clear to go home and miss L and baby could be discharged, by the time I know what's going on the security is now stopping and questioning me and my bro in a manner like we were not entitled to be here so then I started to feel disrespected and my brother managed to calm the situation down before it got out of hand but also felt like it was totally shocking and disrespectful that we were asked along with my one-year-old son to leave the building I couldn't believe it they had ruined our moment our whole experience was short lived miss L felt so disrespected and so did I .... then one day I had a call form miss L sounding upset and frantic eventually after managing to get words out properly she explained to me that someone had phoned the social workers on her a few times previous and now it had happened again she said that they were coming to the house to remove the children and needed her consent to sign some papers I told her "don't answer the door to them "and "tell them where to go" I worked as customer service rep at the time in Sutton Coldfield making appointments for an alarm and security company I told her I would call her after work but that just left me frantic and to a point where I couldn't concentrate, later on that day I called miss L and she had informed me that police had been to the property with the social workers to remove the children I couldn't understand what was going on as miss L in my eyes was a good mom with a good heart she had a few kids previous and at times were a handful but nothing to the point where she couldn't cope she was a good mom with the children she did the best she could under her circumstances. She had told me things in secrecy, and it made me love her more in a feeling sorry for her type of way, but things then grew into an emotional connection I feel we connected because I had experience similar stuff in my life and I could relate to a lot of the things she told me, plus she gave me 2 beautiful kids that I loved and she loved too.

CHAPTER 13

THE PROCESS

I hadn't known that previous to this the social workers were already a main factor in her life before I had been released from prison, she told me that the kids had been removed and that I was to phone the social workers I was so angry at the time when I phoned them I wasn't even listening to anything the woman was saying I was so angry and upset and just wanted to rip their heads off, I agreed that I would have a sit down meeting with the social worker to discuss as they would say the next steps going forward. I remember the day of the meeting I got there 20 minutes early I was so anxious I just wanted to get the meeting stared, I was informed that the kids have been removed and that I had to go through a psychological and psychiatrist test that had been paid for me to attend, it cost 7,000 I had never done one before so I really didn't know what to expect on the day of the test I was called into a room and a woman about 60 sat in the room and gave me certain questions to answer and certain scenarios to work out a solution to it was a 3 hour test and I was so nervous from start to finish after I finished I was asked to hand in my papers and leave and I would be notified by at a later date how I did, weeks came and I couldn't concentrate at work this was all taking a major effect on my life, I eventually told my manager what I was experience as I couldn't hide it any longer she could also notice that I wasn't coming into work with that same happy spark that I usually brought to work in fact I burst into tear and then she also opened up and confided in me that she had also experienced similar to what I was going through, after a nice chat that seem to make me feel better I finally got home to receive my results from the psychological test I had passed and then had to attend my first hearing of court about finding a way to get full custody of my children after the first hearing I would then go back to work and then would have to go to a contact centre 2x a week so I could see my kids this is one of the hardest things I've had to do there would be too assistants in the room observing everything I said and did with the kids while I had contact at times it was really uncomfortable having them their watching my every step and move I would always bring food that I had made that day and prepped so I was always well prepared the contract workers were well impressed with me and told me to keep up what I was doing you're a good dad they said I felt like that was a bit patronising plus all the time I was there, there was never a time where I never wanted to just pick my kids up and run through the door with them and never come back. After leaving the contact centre I was finding it hard to let go of my kids and they were crying "dad dad dad" I couldn't hold it together the social worker finally parted them away from me and took me into a side room as the escorted the kids down the corridor to an awaiting car I could hear there little cries and I felt helpless and hopeless after entering the room she shut the door behind me and the social worker starts to inform me that she might have to cut my contact if I can't hold my emotions together because according to her I was emotionally affecting my kids by crying, I couldn't believe what I was hearing, I somehow managed to hold my composure I don't know how but somehow I did, Between the court case hearings and work I also started to attend dad classes and doing parent courses like understanding kids behaviour and the mind of a child and read various books and completed many more courses, I met so many people that had different stories It made me feel like I was not alone I would attend this regular and have a lot of discussions amongst the dads groups about various help we could give each other. I remember one of the dads telling me that he struggles to do his 3 daughters' hairs in the morning for school, so he used a vacuum to help get their ponytails perfect and it worked I went home and tried it the same day. But it was refreshing to be around such a group at the time I had nowhere to sleep so I was in between stopping at my uncle b house and a friend called Tracy she really looked out for me and while living there I was able to make foods for the kids for contact and prepare myself much better I also had somewhere to sleep and we had a really good friendship she was a good hearted woman and looked out for a lot of people and I was grateful for her for that I was able to build up some stability.

This is my uncleB my dad's brother! When I was about 12 me and my brothers would listen to my uncleB Lewi, Hedgehog, Chello, Zola ranks they had a sound and me and my brother would continuously play them until we knew all of their words my uncleB had this song called PUNANI! Which was a classic amongst the street and family so I feel like they played an influential part in me taking up writing music and being an MC .. plus my uncleB and Aunty P offered me not just support but balance and stability for a time .. my uncleB was the voice of reason everything he said always seem to have you thinking to yourself .. he would always give words of wisdom I spent a lot of time living in my uncles conservatory uncle I was in a situation to get myself together .. that's something I will never forget and because of my uncleB and his wife Aunty P I was able to get my life on the right track, without fail everyday my uncle would be in the kitchen cooking up something, he way me made bakes (which is fried dumplings) was like nothing I've tasted he just seemed to get them perfect everytime .. I watched and learned a lot off my uncleB and others loved and respected him so I will always hold a special place in my heart for my uncleB and aunty P.

I then started a counselling course and also started receiving counselling also I had never really done anything like this before but I started it so it was all new to me my first session was a little awkward but then after a while I built up enough confidence and trust to begin opening up on some of my issues, my counsellor once said to me that as I was speaking about my problems I actually sounded like a therapist.. just after a year of receiving counselling I felt a lot better within myself that someone actually just sat there and listened and didn't judge me and didn't make me feel down and sad it helped me to express myself and ease my mind from the things that were manifesting and damaging me inside I was happy how counselling had helped me and I wanted to do the same and help others. I attended more parent courses and completed more contact sessions. I never tuned up to contact without food that I had already prepped and prepared with love. my third assessment came about 1 year after my kids were taken into care, by now I don't even know how I was getting by I guess it was just the pure determination and love I had inside me, I remember the assessment was set in a bungalow and what it was. was there were going to be a panel of students and assessors that were going to assess me during my contact session with the kids but It was a whole day and they never spoke all the did was just sit with clip boards and watched me carry out my duties I would be lying if I said I didn't feel pressure because I did I remember putting my son in his high chair for lunch and from the moment I put him in he was upset and started throwing his food on the floor" aww come on son open wide" I said as I tried to remain focus on making sure my son was eating but he was still throwing food and his bottle onto the floor I turned it into a game and kept saying things like "ooopsy daisy" you dropped it again" and he would laugh and giggle like it was a game but with the panel watching I thought that I had failed miserably and I also had my daughter who was only 6 months at the time who I had to change her nappies and feeds her also and I managed to do that and show that I could remain calm and composed like a parent it was just strange that assessors were actually here to watch me parent my own kids I found it patronising to say the least but it was challenging and with the panel of assessors there to just make it even worse as far as pressure but I adapted and just did what my heart told me, after I had settled the kids and they were now taking an nap I was called into the main room where all the assessors were and asked how I thought I got on I wasn't sure but I said "yeh good I felt alright" it was then that one of the assessors stood up and "said in all my years working in this industry we have never scored anyone above the average of 5-10 but they were happy to score me a 9 the fact that she did that on record was excellent for me and I was feeling so proud of myself at the time and broke down in tears right after the decision, one the assessors said "do you need some time are you alright " I said yes I'm fine but inside I was just a barrel of emotions, after that moment I thanked the assessors for their time and for the rest of the day I was in my element, weeks after that I was called back to court for the latest update on my battle for full custody of my 2 kids the judge was impressed with the work that I was doing and told me "keep doing what you're doing its very impressive but still I felt like he was patronising me but it was the procedure I had to get through if I was to get the results I so badly wanted I left the court and continued to research as much information on kids in care, single dads. I quickly came to the conclusion that support for single fathers/Men was slim to none of that matter in the uk alone I found their were centres better equipped for single women or women experiencing any kind of abuse which I support with my heart and I respect the women that benefit from these centres because I think they are important and are much needed but with men I felt like there just wasn't enough overall done for single fathers I started researching and making calls attending single moms groups also so I could pick up as much information as I could to prepare myself in the best way possible! I quickly realised that there was only 1-75 centers equipped to deal with men and single fathers and that was in Scotland so I was left to figure it out for myself and with some support from my social worker we spent a lot of time together she would pop up unannounced and announced at times to check how I was dealing with everything a lot of times we use to talk we would end up just leading into other conversations about life in general! One night while I was at home I had just put the kids to bed and was about to watch some tv when my social worker at the time passed by unannounced to inform me I had some papers to fill in and sign she came in and we got talking over a coffee I could smell alcohol on her but at the time I never really gave it a thought! After hours of talking on the sofa my social worker leaned in close towards me and before we knew it we had got into a situation that I never saw coming after it was over I sat quietly on the side and she smiled and said "Bad boy you are"! I was still a bit in no mans land I think the adrenaline was still in me she finally left and that was that I didn't know what to think I left it until she passed by again the next day to talk to me about what had happened and she seemed like she was telling me not to mention nothing as it would jeopardise her position but she still wanted to see me when I had time I guess I went along with it for a while she helped me with money and support I mean she helped me to apply for grants from churches and funding and I will always be grateful to her for that has it helped me on my journey towards settling with my kids while all this was going on I was also researching more but then one day I had a call and my social worker wanted to talk she said "are you home I said yes what's up" she said she was on her way, when she finally arrived she had a glump look on her face and I could tell it was something that wasn't good news, after a coffee and a long pause she managed to mutter the words "im pregnant" I couldn't believe it , I was in shock I then thought she was coming to tell me that she was booking a termination but she was coming to tell me that she was keeping the baby and moving away and that I wasn't tell anyone about the baby I couldn't make this up if I tried .. sure enough 9 months later I receive a message on my phone when I open the message it's a picture of a little baby girl with the message "She's your say hello to Lilly" I hadn't had no contact and thought best I respect what she wanted but one day if my daughters reading this I wanted her to understand daddy's situation in why I'm absent from her life so that she don't grow up wondering and overthinking if daddy loved her x well the answer to that is yes always I think of her but I guess only time will tell as now she would be 2 years younger than my oldest daughter x plus I was still attending the dads classes so I was sharing and gathering information from the groups, also I would often see some of the dads from the groups at the same contact centres I went to and the court hearings I attended as we were all going through similar battles, I was going back and forth to court every other couple of weeks It was mentally draining, but I knew what the vision was and what it would take I would often cry myself to sleep and feel like a right failure I got really low at times and almost felt like just giving up and ending it all the pain inside was something that I couldn't describe in words.

I tried not to go out unless I was going to a contact session, I just didn't want to go outside I felt like everyone had their eyes on me, whenever I was low or sad I would always confide in Tracey it was nice to have such a nice person who understood me and at the time having her around was good for my mental strength because she always encouraged me and made me believe that I could do it. Not only did she offer me stability she also was always there if I needed advice, or I needed to let some stuff of my chest and would always value her friendship and appreciate everything that she done for me. In Fact she helped me prepare myself for court little things like just how to present myself and remain calm and stuff I started having more contact as I was getting closer to my final hearing I was spending a lot more time with my kids and I was even taking them out to the ball pits and stuff and just having fun I was preparing myself for full time parenthood, I got myself my own place which I was lucky enough to get through private renting and at the time the landlord had took into consideration what I was going through and opted to allow me to just give him the deposit and not to worry about giving him a month in advance. just over 15 months had gone, I was so grateful and happy I was more than overjoyed. I remember moving into a new area as the social worker had gave me a map and had informed me that if I wanted to have a chance of being considered to have my kids that I would have to move completely out of the county, I never forget I remember sitting thinking to myself "they trying to make it hard for me" but I told myself that I had done too much and come too far to start turning back now, this was just another hurdle that I would have to overcome, I knew I could do it I just was scared to trust the process, finally the day had come to attend the final hearing. I was so nervous I remember feeling anxious, but I felt like I had done all I could and no matter what. it was all down to the judge's decision. I had endured so much time of my life in front of a judge that majority of the time I always seem to be on the wrong end of judges' decisions.

After hours of going through terms and conditions and everyone had spoken I was finally awarded full custody of my kids, miss L had also spoke and had her say and agreed and also thought that I was capable and the best person for the kids to remain with and I had her full 100% approval, that was also a big weight lifted off my head because the last thing I wanted was us going back and forth in the courtroom with each other, after floods of emotions and tears in the courtroom I contained myself enough to say thank you to the judge and left the building to get ready for the return of my children, I remember I had to get back to my property to get it ready for when they came home for the first time, I brought beds painted the rooms carpet and put some photos on the wall and tried to get it best I could but I was happy with what I had managed to do on my own, the first day had come when they were finally home, I was so emotional I just couldn't contain myself part of me felt like I had let them down and I had a lot of making up to do to them but they were only 3 and 2 so I don't know what was going on in their little minds, I just went with my heart, I didn't have no real experience at the time I just did what seem to come natural to me at the time, so I was ready for whatever was going to be thrown at me, the first week I felt like I had lost a stone in weight I was literally drained and tired I realised quickly that there was just not enough hours in a day and my routine was now changed as far as sleep I don't think I endured a good night's sleep as I was always half asleep just in case I heard a noise and one of them had woke up and needed me. I remember having to sleep right next to my daughters cot whenever I would settle her to sleep I think she felt the presents of me not being in the room and could always sense if I was not in the room so half way through the night I would just put her nest to me in bed where she seemed to sleep better but I would remain awake I was I to scared to fall asleep at the time in case I never heard her cries or rolled over and hurt her so I would always have a pillow either side of her to keep her protected and I would be on the opposite side facing her as she slept peacefully, I realised it was that I gave all I had in my heart and that now my to kids were my main priority and nothing else, I manged to save up and obtain a double buggy so it would help me get to and from the shop a bit easier as both was not fully walking that strongly at the time so I managed to buy a double pushchair so I could take the kids to the park and if they fell asleep I wouldn't have the difficulties of having to carry them both back in my arms so it was really convenient that I had brought one, one day we had been the park and started to rain so I manged to make it home before it got really bad so when I got home I folded the pushchair up as normal but as It was soaking wet I left it outside my front door to eventually dry off the next day when I opened my front door the pushchair had been stolen I was so upset as at the time I hadn't had any more money to just buy another one immediately, I remember thinking to myself "how could anyone steal someone's pushchair" they don't even know my situation how could they " I had only been living in the area about 6 months and I had already felt like I had had my wits tested but I was determined not to be broken or let it brake me, my children were only young at the time so they were 100% dependent and reliant on me and at the time all I really had was myself, I spent many nights watching my kids as they slept, It became something that I would do regular just sit there and watch their innocent faces as they slept it would make me smile, I never loved anything near my kids before the feeling I had was just different to anything id ever encountered you could say I just felt loved 10 times over. My routine consisted on waking up about 6am doing the bottles coming back upstairs changing my daughter and sons nappies then feeding both their bottles to then have to entertain them for the duration of the morning until they were both ready for their 12pm nap which is when I would prepare lunch while they both sleep for about 1 hour each then when both would be awake I would then have to put my son in his high chair as he was more stable being a year older and I would feed him while I would have my daughter in my arms feeding her too I quickly learnt to multitask and by 3pm I would be watching tv or just playing with the kids in the garden, I then would start preparing food for them around 4 so it was ready for around 5:30 but this would while both kids would be wide awake and sometimes full of energy so I would have to read a book them while I peeled the potatoes or I would put my son in his play pen while my daughter was in her bouncer while I prepared the rest of the dinner but it wasn't long before I would have to take her out of there as she loved me picking her up and I think I got into a habit of picking her up so that was all she ever wanted., She was quickly becoming a daddy's girl.

I managed to get my son enrolled into a nursery that wasn't too far from where I moved to the nursery was really good and helped to develop him in many ways, Plus he had fun he made some friends and really enjoyed it there While my son was in nursery It gave me the opportunity and time to spend some quality one and one time with my daughter, singing to nursery rhymes reading books using play dough and watching cartoons, often the social worker would pop in to check how I was coping and how to see how the kids were settling they had to do this for the first 3 months and then they were signed off and I was left to concentrate on building my life with my kids without the feeling of a social worker over my head first I really thought my social worker was against me and I used to think that he was going to work against me and try to take my kids but I was wrong he actually believed in me the whole time in fact it was himself that had to write a final statement to the assessor's on me to the judge and he supported me more than I could thank him for, I was sometimes able to get a nap in between for about 1hour while my daughter took an afternoon nap and my son was at nursery but most nights I would say I never really managed to finally get to sleep until about 11pm and that was if I was lucky and one of my kids hadn't woke up for a nappy change or a bottle or just crying because they were both teething at the time I mean just as my son had finished teething my daughter was just going through the early stages and I would say that these were some of the hardest nights to even think about having a sleep. Though I had moved in my property I was still going to Tracey's to see how she was and she would help drop some of my belongings to my property that I had left while I was living at her house I remember one day we were on the way from her house to drop me and some belongings back home and 10 minutes into the journey her 2 sons had got into an argument in the car I remember Tracy pulling over into MacDonalds carpark and us both calming the boys down, finally after they were calm we decided to grab a MacDonalds and continue on the day, I remember getting out the car and instantly noticing a woman looking straight at me like she knew me I reactivity looked as I was walking towards the door of MacDonalds she approached me and said "I'm sure I know you from somewhere are you one of the twins" I asked her what she meant by that and she said she had heard a lot about me and my twin. I replied with I hope it's good she smiled in a cheeky way before we exchanged socials but didn't exchanged numbers later that month she contacted me and asked if I was busy we had been talking now for about 3 months I said I didn't get out much as I have 2 children that I was full time with on my own, at first I don't think she believed me, we continued talking and messaging most times she would phone me from work as she used to work at her mom's café so she would literally be on the phone to me while she was serving customers until we could both find a suitable day where we could meet up and go on a date, as she also had 2 children prior to meeting me and it wasn't easy to get a free weekend especially while having responsibilities that came first and I respected that about her and that she was a very good hands on mom, we eventually went on a first date and we hit it off instantly I made her laugh she made me laugh she was loud and very chattery and I liked that about her it made me more attracted to her besides the fact that she was beautiful looking. After a few dates and messages and phone calls she finally met my 2 kids and she loved them from the start I was really appreciative for the advice and support she gave me as I was a new dad and times I didn't know it all so she would always give me advice and show me how to do certain things if I wasn't sure there were.

Sometimes I would be awoken from screams because the kids tooth had started coming cutting through and it's just the process that they had to endure but never the less it was so upsetting seeing your own child crying in pain and you feel hopeless but miss k advised me to buy bonjella from the chemist and use that on the kids gums before they go to sleep in fact I think she had come and brought me some down as she was driving at the time so there was times where she would bring over food that she had cooked she cooked a lovely curry I don't think I had ever tasted anyone that makes a better chicken curry than miss k she just knew how to get that perfect she was a very good cook we use to have little cook off's and she would always say "you know my chicken is fire you can't touch my cooking O" she was right but I would never admit it I would just smile but it made me a better cook and I was happy to try and learn things in order to get better she also supported me with the kids when she could I remember her putting bonjella on their little gums and cuddling my daughter with comfort until she was back settled again and I thought that was really cute. I would say probably 2-3 times through the night the kids would wake up screaming in pain I managed to prepare myself by stacking up on bonjella and creams and stuff for their new teeth and it did really help because I was more prepared and miss k had taught me that whenever she wasn't here to put it on their gums 1 hour before they go to sleep and allow it to settle in their gums and this seemed to help a lot I could never tell how much pain it was that they were actually feeling but all I know that I never liked it for them both it really made me emotional at times, eventually they both got through that stage and seemed to sleep through the night pretty well, I mean from about 6am they would both be awake and dependent on me until they were both settled and asleep in bed by 7:45 so by the time I cleaned up and then had a bath and finally get to my bed it was not until around 11pm until I was actually near enough asleep, finally weeks, month went by and the social workers was finally out of my life and I felt like I was ready to focus on my priorities properly. My daughter was also took in by the nursery and that helped me out a lot because she was only 2 at the time and wasn't ready for nursery until another 2 years but the lady that owned the private nursery had saw that I was a single dad and offered to have my daughter for a couple of hours so that I could have some time to myself, I was very appreciative of that and started to take both kids into nursery at 12:30 until 3:00pm I was able to prep dinner wash some clothes and even get a long overdue nap and get a lot more done without having to worry about the children being under my feet for a few hours so I routine myself around the kids finishing nursery at 3 and by then I usually had everything prepared I sometimes had time to go to the gym and was also able to get some shopping done while I had some free time, I felt a lot better because I had time to do stuff and my kids were developing at nursery really well, I literally felt so alone and isolated not only had I moved out my area where I grew up my neighbour didn't speak a word of English and I was on the end house so being on the end meant I never had another neighbour the other side of my home and miss k didn't live that close to mine so whenever she wasn't around I just got on with it and stayed in my routine. So many times when the kids were in bed I would do a lot of over thinking I would often question myself and ask myself can I do this I just wanted everything to be ok and didn't really have much reassurance from anyone so I had to mostly rely on my self-belief and my love for my children, I wrote music in my spare time and managed to book hours in the studio when the kids were at nursery I would work on my album daily I would continuously write any chance I got it was stressful at times a as I was trying to fit it all in as I was being a full time dad too so at times I was mentally drained I would get writers block where I was just mind blocked where I couldn't put my song words together. There were times where I was so tired juggling everything I think I was running off adrenaline, I continued to attend parent courses and decided to build a library under my stairs because I loved reading books and researching things I learnt something new every day, and also the children loved the books and I loved reading to them I brought all my idol 2pac books and always told myself one day that I wanted to have a book out to sit right next to his and that would be a big accomplishment for me, he truly was my inspiration, I feel revisiting stuff I thought I had put to the back of my mind was hard to deal with at times but it also helped me to reflect on what I had been through and how far I had come.

I eventually met miss k parents and they were really nice people I will always have a lot of love and respect for them when they found out that I was a single dad raising my kids on my own they helped me more than anyone that I had met in my entire life they not only brought the kids Christmas presents and birthday presents and easter eggs they supported mentally and made me feel welcomed they treated me like I was part of their family her dad was someone that I could go to for advice on anything and I mean anything and he just seemed to have the answer to whatever the solution was. I had a lot of respect for him also because he showed me how to raise a family and how to show love and always praise your kids and I always remember him telling me "O always be aware of your surroundings and how you act around your kids and the people you have around you will be a reflection of who you are" he taught me things that helped me to become a better parent and better man and I appreciated everything he told me and taught me, he was a real stand up respected man that was all about his family and the kids loved him so much, her mom was a special kind of woman someone that probably only comes around once in a life time she had a great sense of humour and was so down to earth, we use to talk a lot she was also very supportive if ever I needed advice but she was just different she was caring loving and just had a beautiful soul I would always buy her little goodies she loved custard tarts and dairy box of chocolates I would always buy her some whenever I would visit miss k and the occasional bottle of white wine as she lived next door to her parents which was very convenient, I remember her buy me a Newcastle shirt with name on the back and me being a Newcastle united supporter I was so shocked but so grateful for it and she was very supportive to miss k I sometimes questioned why my own parents wasn't like this with my kids and me but it was just what it was and I was grateful to just be around such a lovely set of people that made me look at my life different. I eventually had 2 kids for miss k a boy (Romario) and a girl(janaia) and I was at the heights of love. before having our daughter, we had tragically lost a baby before that which had a major impact on me and miss k and for a while at times things were stressful and sensitive. We had a few fiery moments but honestly because we were both quite loud and emotional and sensitive, some arguments sounded worse than they were there was never a time in the relationship where I'd ever put my hand on her I think we both just got passionate whenever we were disagreeing, but deep down I loved her off after a few years together we split up and I was devastated deep down but it was the right thing to do at the time because let's just say loyalty was broken and I couldn't no longer cope but because of that I no longer have access to my 2 kids with miss k and I just wish things were different as I man I found myself in a situation where I experienced how hard it is for a man to even gain access to his kids and I just think that men should be protected and supported more.

CHAPTER 14

WHEN OPPORTUNITY COMES KNOCKING

After a few years of being at my property I decided to apply to move council to move back to my county that I had originally grown up in, I felt like I was at a stage in my life where I was stable but being around my family and friends would give me that extra little stability and both my kids were also growing up. After a couple of months awaiting the answer to my application, I was finally put into a 3 bed property but it was only temporary accommodation in smith's wood and it was a ground floor flat but it was ok and I was told that I wouldn't be in their long so for the meantime that was mine and my kids new home, I continued my routine with the kids but now I had to settle them into a new home new rooms plus it was only temporary so I would use the time to prepare myself for when I finally got a home that we could settle into permanently, it was the 3rd time I had moved around in 3 years it did have an effect on me mentally and physically and overall at times you could see how drained I was at times I had to re-register both my kids into new schools and get them prepared for a new environment. I constantly worried inside I worried about what people thought of me I would worry about how my kids were feeling with all these sudden changes, I worried about coping I had to start looking at the positives that was going on in my life, and I had to bear all the weight on my shoulders and be strong not only for me but for my kids too. Gradually after I had settled with my kids, I had the opportunity of work but not only that it was working with young ppl my friend who went by the name kadz that offered me the opportunity knew how much working with young ppl was close to my heart so she had kept me in mind when she had set up her own organisation, she reminded me a bit of myself in a sense of she was always helping someone no matter how big or small the matter seemed she always give out positive energy, plus she was my friend I had previously formed a friendship with her through collaborating with some music years prior she was a really good rapper and a good woman she always carried herself well and had a lot of respect from others anywhere I went with her and that made her unique in what she did, she had a good way with words she would always give me words of encouragement like "you're an amazing dad" and to keep trying your best "I'm proud of you" I think the words hit home more because it was coming from someone that I had a lot of respect for. I had to go through a D.B.S. check but once that was cleared, I was able to enjoy learning and working with young ppl it was more like a summer camp in the holidays for when kids were off school, and parents needed their children to have some form of activities to do so I think it was a good project and I admired her for that. Plus I could also see the positive impact it had on all the young ppl that attended it was so refreshing, I was just happy to be part of it and just happy to be able to offer my help wherever I could plus she could see that I was trying to help myself make changes in my own life, what I respect about her is that she didn't have to offer me the opportunity she could of found someone else or anyone else so the fact that she kept me in mind to even be considered I respected her more for that. I learnt so much off the kids and at times was designated to teach a small group which was amazing so many I interacted with so many clever kids it made me think to myself that I would have appreciated something like this when I was young, in the holidays. After the projects was over I looked into setting up my own showcases through my association with music and the links that I had I felt like I could set up my own showcases to try to help young ppl to express themselves and their talents to their local communities it was one thing that I always thought was missing it's like the community's had lost the community spirit and there was little to no opportunity for the young kids so I decided to put shows cases on for my community, all out of my own resources and connections every couple of months I think also working with my friend and being around what she had tried to build herself inspired me to give back more especially to the young generation. I feel it made me open my mind more on a different level, so I was forever grateful. I have been running my showcases years on and they have been a success I also run my own projects for young people who find expressing themselves in an artistic way instead of a verbal way and be creative as that is where I feel that I could make a difference and have a major positive impact on our future generation, I love seeing people passionate about what they are doing and I believe that is what is the drive behind success I think once your passion goes for something that's when I think you should consider a different option because as a child when u develop a passion for something you do it more for the happiness the feeling you have inside and the appreciation of others make you feel confident enough to have that extra belief not necessary the money but when you develop in age the rolls actually reverse and now it's more about the money instead of the passion so I feel it's about trying to find the right balance, But I have a passion for success and to see others succeed. my aim was if I could just help one young kid to chase their dreams or just help to restore belief in them or a father who has no belief in himself being a good dad then I would consider my self-satisfied with that because at the end of the day I felt like I had my brain sparked by my idol so it's only right that I would try to do the same thing and help someone or others. I realise that every day we walk past and interact with people daily and never know the kind of life that they have endured It made me realise that you never really know anyone until you know them. I hope someone can take some inspiration out of my book and find some comfort or some motivation from it or relate to it in some kind of way because everyone has a story this is just mine .... RESPECT IT!

Afterword

While writing this book my first kids mother miss L sadly passed away...

How to follow or contact or book Owen Williams (ElementOG)

Element OG (Facebook)
elementog9 (TikTok)
Elementog og (YouTube music channel)
Elementog_og (Instagram)
og56@live.co.uk (email)